U.S. ENERGY POLICY:
A PRIMER

THE AEI
NATIONAL ENERGY PROJECT

The American Enterprise Institute's
National Energy Project was established in early 1974
to examine the broad array of issues
affecting U.S. energy needs and supplies.
The project will commission research into all important
ramifications of the energy problem—economic
and political, domestic and international, private
and public—and will present the results
in studies such as this one.
In addition it will sponsor symposia, debates, conferences,
and workshops, some of which will be televised.

The project is chaired by Melvin R. Laird,
former congressman, secretary of defense,
and domestic counsellor to the President,
and now senior counsellor of *Reader's Digest*.
An advisory council, representing a wide range of
energy-related viewpoints, has been appointed.
The project director is Edward J. Mitchell,
professor of business economics at
the University of Michigan.

Views expressed are those of the authors
and do not necessarily reflect the views of
either the advisory council and others associated with
the project or of the advisory panels,
staff, officers, and trustees of AEI.

U.S. ENERGY POLICY: A PRIMER

Edward J. Mitchell

American Enterprise Institute for Public Policy Research
Washington, D. C.

Edward J. Mitchell is professor of business economics at the University of Michigan and director of the American Enterprise Institute's National Energy Project.

ISBN 0-8447-3131-5

National Energy Study 1, June 1974

Second Printing, January 1975

Library of Congress Catalog Card No. 74-81456

Printed in the United States of America

CONTENTS

1

ENERGY POLICY
IN PERSPECTIVE

A false perception of the energy problem is common to many experts and the man-in-the-street. Ask Americans what the energy problem is about, and they will probably say it is about shortages: shortages of gasoline, of heating oil, of electricity, of natural gas. Ask a more sophisticated audience, such as oil company executives or government energy officials, and they will express concern about future energy "gaps" as well as current shortages. They will talk of future energy "requirements" or "needs," and how future supply must fall short.

A Shortage Is a Policy

The trouble with these views is that shortages and gaps are not acts of nature that "happen to us"; they are the creations of men, the consequences of deliberate policy choice. Neither smaller supplies nor larger demands imply shortages. In fact, if we never found another barrel of oil or cubic foot of natural gas, or never mined another ton of coal, there would be no necessity for shortages.

This observation follows from the fact that at some price the energy market will clear. As long as either less is demanded or more supplied as price increases, there is some price at which supply equals demand. The matter has been put succinctly by Professor Milton Friedman:

> Economists may not know much. But we do know one thing very well: how to produce shortages and surpluses. Do you want to produce a shortage of any product? Simply have government fix and enforce a legal *maximum* price on the product which is less than the price that would otherwise prevail. . . . Do you want to produce a surplus of any

1

product? Simply have government fix and enforce a legal *minimum* price above the price that would otherwise prevail.[1]

Thus government policy makers always have three options in any market: (1) a market-clearing price, (2) a lower price and shortages, or (3) a higher price and surpluses. There are free-market policies, shortage policies, and surplus policies. The government is now following shortage policies in the energy market. In the 1950s governments (state and federal) elected a surplus policy for oil. In the 1960s they elected a surplus policy for oil and, simultaneously, a shortage policy for natural gas. It will be shown below that in 1965 we had at least 25 percent surplus capacity for producing crude oil, while through the 1960s we had a shortage of natural gas reserve additions on the order of 30 to 60 percent. While these policies may present problems for some consumers and producers—namely, the consumers who are not allocated all they want of the limited supplies and the producers who must hold unwanted surplus capacity or inventories—they are not problems for the government. They are the policies of the government.

There is nothing necessarily irrational about choosing a shortage or a surplus policy over a free-market policy. Like any policy, they have consequences that benefit some and injure others. For example, shortages of gasoline clearly benefit those who receive under rationing all the gasoline they want at less than the free-market price. Those consumers who would like to purchase more gasoline at the free-market price, but cannot, are to that extent worse off. Gasoline suppliers are also worse off. If one is more favorably disposed toward the benefitted group than the injured group, the decision to have shortages is not hard to justify.

Significantly, one group *always* benefits from either a shortage or a surplus policy. A rationing procedure must always be established to allocate a shortage among consumers or a surplus among producers, and the power to influence these rationing decisions is of considerable value. Thus, politicians, bureaucrats, Washington lawyers, and the communications media are beneficiaries. As a practical matter, the benefits accruing to this group may dominate the decision-making process.

Sometimes rather broad-brush reasons are given for the choice of a shortage policy. For example, free-market prices are not being allowed in the gasoline market because, it is said, this would hurt

---

[1] Milton Friedman and Robert V. Roosa, *The Balance of Payments: Free Versus Fixed Exchange Rates* (Washington, D. C.: American Enterprise Institute, 1967), p. 1.

the poor. This implies that the shortage option is better for the poor. Yet there does not appear to be the same degree of support among self-professed supporters of the poor for bread or milk shortages. Such shortages, by this reasoning, favor the poor even more than gasoline shortages. Furthermore, the poor consume such a small proportion of energy supplies that it is rather odd to suggest choosing energy policies primarily for their benefit. Direct assistance to the poor to alleviate their poverty would be more sensible.

It is also argued that a low price, or energy shortage, policy will help reduce inflation. By fighting inflation one can only mean maintaining the purchasing power of the dollar. From our gasoline example it is clear that those allocated all they want at lower prices find their dollars enhanced in value, but those without all they want find their dollars worth less insofar as gasoline is concerned. In what sense can it be said that *the* purchasing power of money is maintained? Unfortunately, in these circumstances the consumer price index reflects only the values of the enhanced dollars. This is an important reason why politicians choose shortages during periods of inflation.

Surely the most remarkable aspect of shortage policies is that many who support the choice of a shortage policy also claim that the shortage is the problem. In particular, many politicians urge prices below the market-clearing level and then bemoan the resulting shortage.[2] If we take them at their word, this implies that they do not know the consequences of their actions. If we do not take them at their word we must concede deception. Whichever is the case, shortage policies are usually not long-lived. Consumers and voters seem to regard them as measures necessary in an emergency that become intolerable after awhile.

Surplus policies, such as the crude oil surplus of the 1950s and '60s, seem to be blessed with greater longevity. One reason is that it is much easier to calculate the distribution of benefits and injuries on the supply side. Businessmen can readily measure in dollars and cents the effects of different prices and different allocation formulas. The difficulties of calculating benefits and injuries of shortage policies to consumers cannot be understated. We know that if the price is set only a little below the market-clearing level the number of consumer beneficiaries will be large but the benefits to each will be small. As the price is lowered individual benefits increase but the number of beneficiaries shrinks as the supply decreases. With demand and supply shifting all the time it becomes very hard for a politician

---

[2] For example, the National Energy Emergency Act of 1973 (S. 2589) labels the shortage as the problem.

or bureaucrat to fine tune the price and allocation formula to his constituents' interest.[3] In the case of surplus policies he has unlimited technical assistance from the cartel he has created.

An important exception to the factors tending to cause shortage policies to be short-lived is the fact that there may be substantial benefits from a shortage policy to suppliers of competing products. If there are close substitutes for a particular product, a shortage policy for that product increases the demand for the substitutes. This is what has happened in the natural gas market. Prices far below the market-clearing level for natural gas are creating artificial demands for liquified natural gas (LNG) and synthetic gas from coal, both of which cost at least double the probable market-clearing price. Strong opposition to deregulation of natural gas prices in 1972 executive branch discussions came only from those associated with LNG interests. And the principal Senate advocate of stricter and more extensive price regulation of natural gas is from the state with the largest bituminous coal resources.

Thus, while there is little likelihood of a long-run shortage policy on energy, there is a good probability of deliberate shortage policies for specific forms of energy. Many new forms of energy, such as synthetic fuels from coal, have a chance for commercial success only if shortage policies are imposed on competing cheaper sources, such as conventional oil and natural gas.

Is Energy Scarcity Increasing?

Abandoning shortage policies will mean higher prices. For awhile these prices will be higher than would have existed had free-market policies been chosen all along and higher than the level that will prevail in the long run. Supply in today's market is geared to the prices expected under a shortage policy. And, unfortunately, it takes several years for energy supplies to respond to price. In a free market everyone can have all he wants at the market price. There are no gaps or shortages. The true measure of scarcity, therefore, is price, and the measure of long-run scarcity is long-run price. The prices we will observe immediately when the free market is reinstated will overstate the long-run scarcity of energy.

The question that seems to concern many is whether energy is getting so scarce that severe adjustments will have to be made in the

---

[3] The problem of creating and sustaining consumer coalitions is discussed in Sam Peltzman, "Pricing in Public and Private Enterprises: Electric Utilities in the United States," *The Journal of Law and Economics*, vol. 14, no. 1 (April 1971).

way we live. This concern is not focused on the scarcity of oil-refining or electric-power-generating capacity, both of which have been giving us problems recently. We know these are basically manufacturing activities and are subject to no more scarcity in the long run than plants that produce automobiles or sewing machines. The concern is about the raw materials for these plants—oil, natural gas, coal, and uranium. Are we depleting these natural resources so fast that we will run out before long? Many think so.

If the age of an idea contributes to its validity then the doomsday thesis has a lot going for it. However, the doomsayers have not only been consistently vocal, they have also been consistently wrong. America has had less than a dozen years' supply of oil left for a hundred years. In 1866 the United States Revenue Commission was concerned about having synthetics available when crude oil production ended; in 1891 the U.S. Geological Survey assured us there was little chance of oil in Texas; and in 1914 the Bureau of Mines estimated total future U.S. production at 6 billion barrels—we have produced that much oil every twenty months for years. Perhaps the most curious thing about these forecasts is a tendency for remaining resources to grow as we deplete existing resources. Thus, a geologist for the world's largest oil company estimated potential U.S. reserves at 110 to 165 billion barrels in 1948. In 1959, after we had consumed almost 30 billion of those barrels, he estimated 391 billion were left.[4]

There are two reasons why these forecasts have been so wrong in the past and why they are so irrelevant today. First, there is the popular tendency to focus on proved reserves, which always appear frighteningly small. Proved reserves in the oil- and gas-producing industry are essentially the same as what are called inventories in other businesses. The fact that oil men hold only ten or fifteen years' supply of oil under the ground should be of as much concern to us as the fact that shoe stores keep only thirty days' supply of shoes on the shelf. To hold more would be unprofitable for the businessman and uneconomical for society. When we do find places, such as the Middle East and North Africa, holding fifty years' supply we are witnessing an error in business judgment, or an expectation of enormous growth of deliveries, or an extremely low cost of holding inventories, or some combination of the three.

When policy makers go beyond proved reserves to estimates of potentially recoverable reserves they often misinterpret the figures.

---

[4] DeGolyer and MacNaughton, "Report on National Energy Policy," privately circulated report, 1971, Table 20.

When geologists say that the United States has 300 or 400 billion barrels of potentially recoverable crude oil—about fifty to seventy years' consumption at current rates—they are assuming *present technology* and *present price levels.*[5] These quantities, as rough as they are, have meaning only if they have a price tag placed on them. But one of the few certainties in an uncertain world is that future technology and future prices will be different. The ultimate quantity of oil under the ground is (as Professor M. A. Adelman tells us) unknown, unknowable, and, most important, uninteresting. The pertinent questions are, How much do we have to give up to get an extra barrel (or billion barrels) of oil? How much is that barrel worth to us? If it is worth more than it costs, and it costs less than alternative energy sources, we should use it; if not, we should leave it in the ground. When we decide to stop using oil it makes no difference whether we have left in the ground an infinite amount, a trillion barrels, or a barrel and a half.

The focus on the very long run by the doomsayers is good strategy. Bad forecasting is rarely dismissed because it is bad; instead, people demand a better forecast. But economists and businessmen understand that no one knows what lies ahead fifty years and that the costs of searching for highly uncertain answers greatly exceeds their value.

Even forecasts of only the next ten to twenty years are of little value. To illustrate this point, consider the forecasts made of 1980 energy consumption in 1962 and in 1971, halfway to the target date. In 1962 the Committee on Interior and Insular Affairs of the United States Senate offered a consensus of eleven forecasts of 1980 energy consumption. Actual 1962 energy consumption, the 1980 consensus forecast, and the increase over 1962 implied by that forecast are shown in Table 1. For comparison, figures for representative 1971 studies are also shown. Table 2 gives the same comparison for projected oil consumption using the same sources.

The more recent forecasts predict an increment in energy consumption 60 to 80 percent larger than earlier forecasts. In the case of oil the more recent forecasts predict increments 70 to 120 percent higher. For perspective, the *difference* between the 1962 Senate Interior Committee consensus forecast of energy consumption and the 1971 Department of the Interior forecast is considerably greater than 1973 U.S. oil production and more than double 1973 U.S. oil

---

[5] Ibid.

Table 1

ENERGY CONSUMPTION FORECASTS, 1962–1980
(quadrillions of British thermal units)

Source	Forecast Date	Actual Consumption 1962	Forecast Consumption 1980	Forecast Increment 1962–1980
Senate Interior Committee[a] (consensus of eleven forecasts)	1962	47.4	82.0	34.6
National Petroleum Council[b]	1971	47.4	102.6	55.2
Department of the Interior[c]	1971	47.4	108.7[d]	61.3

Source:

[a] U.S. Congress, Senate, Committee on Interior and Insular Affairs, *Report of the National Fuels and Energy Study Group on Assessment of Available Information on Energy in the United States*, 87th Congress, 2d session, September 1962.

[b] National Petroleum Council, *U.S. Energy Outlook: An Initial Appraisal, 1971–1985*, vol. 1 (Washington, D.C.: National Petroleum Council, 1971), pp. 13-14.

[c] U.S. Department of the Interior, *United States Energy: A Summary Review* (Washington, D.C.: Government Printing Office, 1972), p. 12.

[d] Interpolated from 1975 and 1980 forecasts assuming constant rate of growth.

Table 2

OIL CONSUMPTION FORECASTS, 1962–1980
(millions of barrels per day)

Source	Forecast Date	Actual Consumption 1962	Forecast Consumption 1980	Forecast Increment 1962–1980
Senate Interior Committee[a]	1962	10.6	16.4	5.8
National Petroleum Council[b]	1971	10.6	23.5	12.9
Department of the Interior[c]	1971	10.6	20.6[d]	10.0

Source: Same as Table 1.

imports. One might also note that the rate of oil consumption forecast by the Interior Committee for 1980 was already achieved in 1972.[6]

---

[6] For a survey of earlier forecasts see Pacific Northwest Laboratories, *A Review and Comparison of Selected United States Energy Forecasts* (Washington, D. C.: Government Printing Office, 1969).

This kind of forecasting performance is clearly uninspiring. More important, there is no reason to believe that we can significantly improve our forecasting accuracy in the future. Changes in tastes, technology, and resource discoveries are so unpredictable as to make ten- or twenty-year forecasts little more than crystal-ball gazing.

Apart from undercutting the doomsday thesis, the inaccuracy of forecasts has great significance for public policy. The notion that government can successfully plan to meet specific future energy "needs" or "requirements" by blueprinting supply programs for oil, coal, and other energy sources over the next decade is pure illusion. *Almost certainly such programs would result in large surpluses or shortages and unnecessary costs.*[7] What *is* called for are institutions that are self-adjusting and responsive to change. The market is one such institution. The political and bureaucratic processes as we know them today are not.

What little we do know about the intermediate future, say 1985 or 1990, does *not* suggest significantly increased energy costs. The world energy market is, of course, dominated by Middle East oil. Adelman, using very conservative figures, sums up the world oil market this way:

> For at least fifteen years we can count on, and must learn to live with, an abundance of oil that can be brought forth from fields now operated in the Persian Gulf at something between 10 and 20 cents per barrel at 1968 prices and in some other provinces at costs even lower when account is taken of transport.[8]

When we turn to the United States, matters are not so simple. We have already mentioned the 300-400 billion barrels estimated, but the "supply curve" of U.S. oil and natural gas is not nearly as flat as the Persian Gulf curve. At any one time a great deal of oil is being produced in the United States at costs of twenty cents per barrel and at costs of $4.00 per barrel. The high-cost barrels must, of course, set the market price. Nevertheless, knowledge of what the average or "typical" barrel might cost does give us a point on the supply curve, and if the "tilt" of that curve does not change greatly, it can tell us something about likely future costs at the margin.

In the early 1930s the average cost (excluding bonuses, royalties, taxes, and other rents) of producing a barrel of U.S. crude oil was

---

[7] One must recognize that surpluses can be just as costly as shortages. Indeed, because of their longevity surpluses might be presumed to be more costly.

[8] M. A. Adelman, *The World Petroleum Market* (Baltimore: Johns Hopkins University Press, 1972), p. 77.

eighty cents.[9] In the early 1960s the cost has been estimated to have been $1.22,[10] and in 1972 another source gives $1.58 for onshore production and $1.51 for offshore Gulf of Mexico production.[11] Since the wholesale price index tripled between the early 1930s and the early 1960s average *real* costs appear to have declined.

We know that most future U.S. production will be offshore or in Alaska. One estimate of future average costs on the outer continental shelf is $1.61 per barrel.[12] The costs of Prudhoe Bay (Alaskan North Slope) crude run about twenty-five cents at the wellhead and no more than $1.25 delivered to the West Coast.[13] Some other Alaskan crude could run higher at the wellhead, but generally it would be closer to market.

Most of the still unproven future reserves appear to be on federal lands. This has an important bearing on whether the costs mentioned above will tend to determine market prices, or whether more marginal sources, say from secondary or tertiary recovery projects, will do so.

The federal government has been extremely reluctant to permit exploitation of petroleum resources on its lands. Naval Petroleum Reserve Number Four, which contains the geological extension of the Prudhoe Bay field, has sat untapped for half a century. The director of Naval Petroleum Reserves believes the U.S. Geological Survey estimate that Reserve Number Four holds 33 billion barrels of crude oil reserves—an amount greater than present "Lower 48" reserves—may prove conservative.[14] Sitting untapped, outside Los Angeles, is the nation's third largest proved oil field—Naval Petroleum Reserve Number Three, the Elk Hills field.

There seems to be no rational explanation for leaving these vast reserves untapped. The House Armed Services Committee, which oversees the naval petroleum reserves, simply has shown no inclination to allow Americans to make use of them. And when an official of the Defense Department recently endorsed exploitation of "Pet 4" by opening it up for competitive bidding, a major television network

---

[9] U.S. Department of the Interior, *Report on the Cost of Producing Crude Petroleum* (Washington, D. C.: Government Printing Office, 1935), and Adelman, *World Petroleum Market.*

[10] Adelman, *World Petroleum Market,* p. 76.

[11] U.S. Department of the Interior, "Questions and Policy Issues Related to Oversight Hearings on the Administration of the Outer Continental Shelf Lands Act," mimeographed, March 1972, pp. 86-87.

[12] Ibid., p. 88.

[13] Calculations by the author, 1971.

[14] *Oil and Gas Journal,* 17 September 1973, pp. 38-39.

saw it as a potential scandal rivalling Teapot Dome because the official held stock in an oil company!

When we turn to natural gas the picture is clearer by virtue of a more extensive cost study, and the picture is bright. We will have much more to say about this later.[15]

The upshot of these cost estimates, plus other supply studies, is that there is an abundance of petroleum likely to be available at moderate costs. The quantity of coal available at near-current real costs is well known.[16] And the long-run supply curve of uranium consistently embarrasses supporters of breeder reactors.[17]

This is not to say that real energy costs will not rise. Rather it -suggests that the incremental barrel of oil might cost double what it has been costing—but *not* five times today's cost. In terms of consumer prices a doubling of the price of oil from the $3.50 per barrel level prevalent in early 1973 to $7.00 per barrel means a little more than eight cents added to the price per gallon of gasoline and heating oil. That implies a roughly 20 percent increase in gasoline price using August 1973 prices as a base. Twenty percent is hardly the kind of change in price that drastically alters lifestyles. In 1964 gasoline consumers in Cheyenne, Wyoming, paid average gasoline prices which were almost 25 percent higher than those paid by consumers in Wichita, Boston, Detroit, and St. Louis.[18] This did not seem to dramatically affect the way they lived.

Indeed much larger differences in energy prices seem to have little recognizable effect on people's lives. It is not uncommon for electric rates to be 50 or 100 percent different from one town to another in the same state. A 250 kilowatt hour electric bill in Pleasantville, New York, is three times that of Plattsburgh, New York, yet does not seem to have resulted in profound differences in living patterns.[19]

This is not to say that energy consumers don't alter energy consumption in response to price changes. The evidence suggests that the consumption response to price changes is substantial. A recent study indicates that a 30 percent change in gasoline consumption could be induced by only a 40 percent change (in the opposite

---

[15] See pages 23-24 and 66-69 below.

[16] U.S. Geological Survey, *Coal Resources of the United States, January 1, 1967* (Washington, D. C.: Government Printing Office, 1969).

[17] National Petroleum Council, *Report of the Nuclear Task Group* (Washington, D. C.: Government Printing Office, 1972), pp. 21-27.

[18] *Platt's Oilgram Price Service* (daily publication by McGraw-Hill), various issues.

[19] Federal Power Commission, *Typical Electric Bills* (Washington, D. C.: Government Printing Office, 1970).

direction) in price. Electricity consumption seems to respond almost proportionately to changes in electric rates.[20] The point is that these adjustments in consumption are not catastrophic. They do not alter noticeably the way people live.

Why an Energy Crisis?

While costs of producing energy have changed over the years, there is no evidence that they have changed so quickly or so dramatically as to bring about the current scarcity. If the supply side is not to blame, what about the demand side? Statistics developed in Appendix A show a significant acceleration in the growth of energy consumption between 1965 and 1970 as compared with the periods 1960 to 1965 and 1955 to 1965. This suggests that a rapidly rising demand for energy might have caused the crisis.

However, the evidence does not support this thesis. For consumption growth to have caused the crisis, its acceleration must have been induced by an exogenous increase in demand. Three pieces of evidence make this unlikely. First, the gross national product actually grew at a slower rate (3.4 percent per annum) from 1965 to 1970 than it did from 1960 to 1965 (5.3 percent) and from 1955 to 1965 (4.1 percent). Since the economy would have to provide the main stimulus for demand growth, how can we explain an acceleration in energy consumption growth alongside a deceleration in economic growth? Second, if we go beyond overall economic growth to search for exogenous factors we do not find them. One serious attempt to attribute accelerating consumption to factors such as declining efficiency of electric plants and the growth of air conditioning—if these could indeed be considered exogenous factors—concedes that only a modest portion of energy consumption growth can be explained in this way.[21]

But most important, an exogenous increase in the rate of demand growth implies rising prices or, at least, less rapidly falling prices. The fact is that real energy prices were falling throughout the 1950s, and the decline accelerated continuously through the 1960s and early '70s right up to the middle of 1973. Real energy prices

---

[20] H. S. Houthakker and P. K. Verleger, "Dynamic Demand Analyses of Selected Energy Resources," a paper delivered to the American Economic Association, December 1973.

[21] National Economic Research Associates, "Energy Consumption and Gross National Product in the United States: An Examination of Recent Changes in the Relationship," privately circulated, March 1971.

Table 3

ENERGY CONSUMPTION, ECONOMIC GROWTH,
AND ENERGY PRICES, 1950–1973

	Average Annual Rate of Change				
	1950–55	1955–60	1960–65	1965–70	1970–mid-1973
Energy consumption: heat index	3.4	2.5	3.9	5.3	n.a.
Energy consumption: value-weighted index	7.7	4.6	4.9	6.2	n.a.
Real gross national product	4.7	2.3	5.3	3.4	n.a.
Index of energy prices	−.62	−.8	−1.3	−1.7	−1.9 a

a Preliminary estimate.
Source: Appendix A.

fell 3.1 percent from 1950 to 1955, 3.7 percent from 1955 to 1960, 6.5 percent from 1960 to 1965, and 8.1 percent from 1965 to 1970. The fall from 1970 to June 1973 extrapolates to a five-year rate of 9.4 percent. Overall, real energy prices fell by about one-fourth between 1950 and the middle of 1973. The figures on energy consumption and prices and economic growth are shown in Table 3. Details may be found in Appendix A.

This price pattern implies that it was not so much exogenous shifts in demand that spurred consumption, but rapidly falling prices inducing consumers to purchase more energy. In short, energy was becoming more and more of a bargain compared to other consumer products—and so consumers bought more.

Everyone knows that since the summer of 1973 many energy prices, particularly for petroleum products, have soared. What we have experienced is an accelerating decline in prices over two decades followed by a sharp upward thrust in the past year. It is clear that changes in energy costs or in the demand for energy cannot account for what has happened. There is only one source of explanation: changes in government policies that have artificially manipulated scarcities in the marketplace.

In the world oil market, prices fell during the 1950s and 1960s, the decline being interrupted only by occasional Middle East crises. This decline was not the result of falling oil production costs but of the weakening ability of exporters to sustain prices above costs.

By 1971 the cartel of producing nations had strengthened its ability to control production and prices. This is the major cause of oil scarcity outside the United States and clearly not the consequence of increased costs or scarcity of supplies. Middle East oil is at least as abundant relative to demand now as it was in 1950.[22]

In the U.S. oil market, state production restrictions, federal import quotas, and a tight federal leasing policy kept oil prices high in the 1950s and mid-1960s. As surplus crude oil capacity declined in the late 1960s, the natural response of a cartel would have been to raise prices. Instead, quotas were liberalized and prices held down, first by informal pressures and the rising quotas, and then by mandatory price controls. The real price of U.S. crude oil fell from 1967 to 1972. While domestic spare capacity was shrinking, public policy shifts dictated more imports and lower prices, stimulating demand and increasing dependence on foreign supplies.

In the United States natural gas prices rose through most of the 1950s. The installation of price ceilings in 1960 kept wellhead prices from rising further. The low ceiling prices increased demand as well as stimulating production out of existing reserves—it was hardly worthwhile to hold reserves for production at a later date if prices were not going to rise. But low gas prices meant declining exploration for new reserves since this was becoming more costly. A shortage of natural gas to consumers was inevitable, although this was hidden for a time by the use of huge reserves accumulated in earlier periods. By 1970 available gas supplies were falling short of demand.

The real cost of generating electric power fell through the 1950s and most of the 1960s. Real prices also fell stimulating consumption. By the late 1960s, however, the decline in production costs was reversed by a slowing in the growth of generating plant efficiency and the added costs of meeting environmental standards. These were not reflected immediately in electric rates, and the prospects for investment in the electric utility industry soured: the rate of return to a stockholder (including dividends and price appreciation) of a typical electrical utility fell to only 1.4 percent over the 1967-1972 period.[23] Capital became difficult to raise, and capacity could not be expanded to meet demand.

---

[22] The ratio of reserves to production in the Middle East and North Africa has been around 50 for the past two decades.

[23] See J. Hass, E. Mitchell, and B. Stone, *Financing the Energy Industry* (Cambridge, Mass.: Ballinger Publishing Co., forthcoming 1974), pp. IV-18-20, and B. Seligman, "What Others Think: The Declining Return on Electric Utility Investment," *Public Utilities Fortnightly*, 9 November 1972, p. 45.

Americans have been induced by changes in public policy to consume more energy. But the domestic public policies that stimulated consumption in the short run discouraged investment in the long run. The year of reckoning was 1973. Almost simultaneously the cartel of oil-producing countries that had previously failed to keep prices up and production down turned things around and raised prices with astounding success.

To the extent that U.S. international policies might have avoided this turnaround, part of the blame must be laid at the door of our policy makers. But even if U.S. policies are not responsible for the success of the oil cartel's price increases, they *can* be blamed for permitting us to become dependent upon the cartel. In 1972 the United States imported 500,000 barrels of crude and oil products per day from Arab countries. The shortfall in natural gas supplies alone—caused by severe Federal Power Commission (FPC) price restrictions—is estimated at the equivalent of 1,800,000 barrels of oil per day in 1972,[24] or three and a half times oil imports from Arab nations. While not all unmet gas demand was converted into additional oil imports, much of it was, since the Persian Gulf producers were the residual energy suppliers to this nation.

The energy crisis is a crisis of public policy. It is the consequence of shortage policies adopted without reference to the public interest. *There is no evidence that in a free energy market anything resembling a crisis, or even a problem, would have occurred.* The notion that these artificial scarcities are due to private conspiracies has no foundation. In spite of decades of investigation by the U.S. Federal Trade Commission and of unending charges by small businessmen, congressmen, and "public interest" law firms, nothing that would have had any significant bearing on market trends in the past couple of decades has been uncovered, the popularity of conspiratorial themes notwithstanding. The petroleum industry in particular has exhibited the major characteristics of a competitive industry.[25] To be sure, inefficiencies in market structure have existed, but these have invariably been the consequence of government policies and laws, not private conspiracies.

---

[24] Paul W. MacAvoy and Robert S. Pindyck, "Alternative Regulatory Policies for Dealing with the Natural Gas Shortage," *Bell Journal of Economics and Management Science*, vol. 4, no. 2 (Autumn 1973), pp. 489–492.

[25] Obviously this is not the kind of issue that can be dealt with adequately here. Nor is there a useful literature on the subject to refer to. For an attempt to expose some of the mythology of "big oil" monopolies see Appendix B. Also see Richard B. Mancke, "Petroleum Conspiracy: A Costly Myth," *Public Policy*, vol. 22, no. 1 (Winter 1974).

The list of government laws, programs, policies, and institutions determining the course of the energy market is long, but only a handful have been crucial. They are: the Mandatory Oil Import Program, the Texas Railroad Commission and market-demand prorationing, the Natural Gas Act and FPC regulation of natural gas prices, the Organization of Petroleum Exporting Countries (particularly certain Arab members), the U.S. Cost of Living Council and price controls, the U.S. Department of the Interior's minerals leasing policy, and the Environmental Protection Agency and the laws it is required to enforce. While other policies have had enormous impact on our pocketbooks—for example, the Atomic Energy Commission's multi-billion dollar research and development efforts in conventional and breeder reactors—they have had negligible effect on the energy market itself. Most of the remainder of this monograph is devoted to certain of the above mentioned government actions.

2

POLICIES WITHOUT CRITERIA: GAPOLOGY

Central to an understanding of the political economy of energy is the knowledge that most publicly oriented energy discussions do not deal seriously with energy markets. To appreciate how the energy debate actually takes place, we must repress our knowledge of how markets work and adopt an approach that might be called "gapology," the theory or science of gaps.

The term derives from the procedure of setting out separately the prospective future demand for energy at *current* prices and comparing this to the estimated future supply of energy at *current* prices. In recent years, this comparison always ends up in a gap, or shortage. In this approach, the jargon of economics is used: "demand," "supply," "consumption," "production," and, in more sophisticated attempts, sometimes even "inventories."

The gap approach is so common that it is doubtful that there is anyone who has looked seriously at the energy question without coming across several gap analyses. Most energy companies follow this approach, but do not leave the gap unfilled—they almost always fill it with imports of overseas oil and liquified natural gas. (With recent Arab cutoffs, it is not clear how this will be handled.)

Government agencies, such as the FPC, usually leave the gap unfilled and forecast a shortage. A good example of the gap approach is to be found in the Department of the Interior's *United States Energy: A Summary Review*.[1] It forecasts energy "requirements" to the year 2000, breaking this down among different fuels. While these estimates take into account such factors as economic activity, population growth, and environmental controls, the only reference to price as a variable determining demand or supply is an analysis

---

[1] Washington, D. C.: Government Printing Office, January 1972.

of the effects of *relative* costs of different fuels on consumption and a comment to the effect that demand is "relatively insensitive to price."[2] The final chapter in the report goes on to consider the various options for filling the gap. In the case of natural gas, the traditional line chart is drawn showing total demand exceeding domestic and Canadian supply after 1975. In the gap on the chart is a series of question marks referring to the various options for filling the gap: liquified natural gas, Canadian gas, Arctic gas, and synthetic gas. While the importance of price in determining future domestic natural gas supplies is clearly noted in the report,[3] no statement is made regarding the price assumed in the projections, nor is there any suggestion that the gap might be closed merely by freeing the price.[4]

Gapological reasoning may also be found in everyday newspaper reports of the energy problem. On 2 December 1973 the *New York Times* ran this headline: "Oil Independence—U.S. Self-sufficiency by 1980 Is Unfeasible," followed by the statement that "most experts feel that, despite our best efforts, the United States is likely to remain dependent upon oil imports to make up the gap between domestic supplies and sharply rising demand."[5] Actually the United States could be self-sufficient tomorrow simply by abolishing all import rights and letting the domestic market clear. All domestic demand would then be met by domestic supply. The United States imports foreign oil not because self-sufficiency is infeasible but because it would be too costly. Whether we will be self-sufficient in the future should be dependent upon the relative costs and risks of foreign and domestic supplies.

Concerning ways to fill the gap the same article notes that "the United States has the world's largest coal resources, which will come increasingly into use as environmentally sound ways to use coal are found." This illustrates a principal feature of gap analysis: the emphasis on the *quantity* of potentially gap-filling resources rather than their *cost*. The quantity of U.S. coal resources is not a great deal more relevant than the quantity of energy emitted by distant stars (which I presume is much greater than that contained in our coal reserves). It is possible that we now consume more coal than we

---

[2] Ibid., pp. 6 and 13.

[3] Ibid., p. 22.

[4] A representative sample of gap analyses would also include the National Petroleum Council's *U.S. Energy Outlook: An Initial Appraisal, 1971-1985*, vols. 1 and 2, and Federal Power Commission, Bureau of Natural Gas, *Natural Gas Supply and Demand, 1971-1990: Staff Report No. 2* (Washington, D. C.: Government Printing Office, February 1972).

[5] *New York Times*, Section 3, p. 1.

ought to taking into account harmful effects on air quality. But finding "environmentally sound" ways to burn coal is not the issue either. The real question is whether it is less costly to burn coal than oil or gas, where cost includes not only the resources used in production but also the injury to people exposed to harmful emissions.

Here is another statement from the same *Times* article: "Many economists would add that projections of demand . . . are based on the assumption that there will be an adequate supply of energy." This statement has meaning only if "demand" means "consumption" and demand and supply are completely insensitive to price. But energy demand and supply are certainly sensitive to price, and therefore the statement is meaningless. If this *Times* article is an accurate representation of how a significant number of energy experts and economists think about energy issues, is it really surprising that there is trouble in the energy markets?

Filling the Gap

Once a gap or shortage has been revealed, the question that inevitably arises is: How do we fill the gap? This becomes the central question of public policy. Clearly, the gap-reducing or eliminating measures fall neatly into two categories: those that reduce demand and those that increase supply. At this point, serious divisions break out in the gapologist camp. Some are very much for reducing demand, for example, environmentalists. Others, such as energy producers, urgently want to increase supply. Thus, when it comes to specific policy recommendations, there is great conflict in the camp—what unites all gapological factions, however, is a similar perception of the problem.

There are several remedies offered to fill the energy gap. On the supply side there is usually talk of government R&D to develop new energy technologies—some even suggest crash programs on the order of the Apollo moon project. Also proposed are tax incentives and laws to remove obstacles to the siting of facilities, new leasing programs for federal lands and even direct federal exploitation of federally controlled resources. The value of each proposal is seen as the extent to which it increases supply.

On the demand side there is talk of eliminating "unnecessary" consumption, of requiring greater insulation in homes, of imposing changes in transportation methods, and of requiring more efficient energy-using equipment. The value of each suggested measure is, of course, the extent to which it reduces consumption.

Now it is obvious that there are numerous combinations of supply-augmenting and demand-reducing measures that will do the job. Each gapologist can choose his own set. Politically this is one of the great virtues of the approach. Each interested party can rank the measures in terms of his own self-interest and choose a unique combination that will do the job while maximizing his own well-being. Of course, one has to be careful to meet the constraints imposed by the game. If all the measures that benefit one personally, or corporately, do not fill the gap, one must go beyond them and choose further measures to close the gap, even though they may not involve personal gain. One must have a complete solution. This is why some parties are willing to back remedies that obviously do not benefit them. (For example, gasoline suppliers sometimes back gasoline taxes.)

The Role of Prices

It is also necessary to show balance. One cannot simply choose from one side of the ledger. Balance shows wisdom and enhances credibility. The President's energy message of April 1973 was widely criticized as unbalanced, favoring the supply over the demand side of the menu.

But what is wrong with this approach? Do we not want to fill the energy gap? Do we prefer shortages? The answer, as explained earlier, lies in the arbitrary assumptions of the analysis. Inevitably, the gapologist assumes that prices will remain at current or near-current levels. Current prices are prices that prevail today. They did not prevail yesterday and will not prevail tomorrow (unless, for some peculiar reason, we force them to).

Why should we project future demand and supply at current prices? Suppose instead we project them at prices three times as high as current prices. We will almost certainly then show a reversal of the gap—a surplus. Gapologists would then have to figure out ways of reducing supply and increasing demand. Indeed, this is the principal activity of gapologists in markets characterized by surplus policies. It was the preoccupation of U.S. oil men, and particularly oil state conservation agencies, until very recently.

A clever gapologist might see that we can create not only shortages and surpluses, we can even find prices that eliminate any gap—that is, that clear the market. And from simply observing markets, he will note that left alone they clear by themselves every day.

One can only conjecture that many gapologists do not really appreciate the fact that at higher prices consumers really do buy less and producers offer more, or that they believe these tendencies are so weak that only astronomical prices will eliminate gaps. This, of course, contradicts all experience in the energy market and numerous economic studies of energy markets. To cite a recent example, in 1970, during the period of severe scarcity of tankers and sharply rising demand for low-sulfur heavy oil, many consumers claimed that they could not find supplies. There was no low-sulfur heavy oil available— there was a shortage or gap, or so the claims went. Actually the government's policy of letting the market operate freely, allowing Americans to compete with foreigners for scarce supplies, permitted the market to clear. Prices did rise sharply. But investigations by the Office of Emergency Preparedness found *none* of over fifty claims of shortage to be valid. Lack of availability turned out to mean lack of availability at the price desired. Furthermore, the new higher prices turned out to be much closer to the long-run trend than the old prices. (The price of low-sulfur heavy oil rose from $2.00 per barrel to a seemingly outrageous $3.50. It is now $10.00 to $13.00.)

This fear of gaps often leads to hysterical and extreme policy positions. Because of the linearity of the analysis we hear talk of "needs" and "requirements" rather than "wants" and "desires." Needs, by definition, must be met, *or else.* This conception of necessity leads to exaggerated metaphors. Oil is no longer a commodity traded in a market; it is the "lifeblood of the nation." The oil shortage means "dramatic changes in lifestyles." Gapologists of all persuasions constantly speak in such urgent phrases.

If one adopts a market-oriented economic approach the problem immediately becomes two-dimensional: at some price the market will clear. We may not like the price at which the market clears, but we know that under different policies the market will clear at different levels. We must then analyze each policy to see what it actually does in the marketplace. A policy will injure some parties and benefit others; it will move the market price higher or lower; it will have a net benefit or cost to the nation and a specific distribution of costs and benefits among individual citizens. Whether we want a particular policy is a matter of preference and values, once we know the costs and benefits and their distribution. This takes us into the world of public choice and preference and out of the realm of necessity and compulsion.

This is not to suggest that energy policy decisions are unimportant. They are extremely important, because the differences in benefits and costs among alternative policies are enormous. But the gap approach to energy policy does not deal with costs and benefits. And many policies that would substantially curtail demand or augment supply—fill the gap—do not have desirable cost-benefit characteristics. Indeed, they may have almost no benefits at all, as the following concrete example illustrates.

Gap-Filling with R&D

To contrast approaches to policy choice, let us consider S. 1283, unanimously passed by the Senate in December 1973 "to establish a national program for research, development, and demonstration in fuels and energy." For a taxpayer cost of $20 billion the bill would establish federal energy corporations to demonstrate technologies for shale oil, coal gasification, advanced cycle power, geothermal steam, and coal liquification. As stated in the bill, its supporters are motivated by the findings that "the Nation is currently suffering a critical shortage of environmentally acceptable forms of energy," the "major reason for this energy shortage is our past and present failure to formulate an aggressive research and development strategy," and "the Nation's critical energy problems can be solved by 1983 if a national commitment is made now to accord the proper priority, to dedicate the necessary financial resources, and to enlist our unequalled scientific and technological capabilities to develop new options and new management systems to serve national needs, conserve vital resources, and protect the environment."

It is evident from the provisions of the bill that "shortage" is seen as the problem. The intellectual rationale for the bill, contained in the Senate Interior Committee's *A Study of Energy Research and Development Prospects and Shortages*,[6] although rather sophisticated, is still just one more argument in favor of filling gaps or shortages as the goal of policy.[7]

The policy criterion of the gap approach is simply that research and development result in the production of energy (which will, of course, help fill the gap). Note that this is a purely technical question, a subject for engineers, not economists or policy analysts. The National Academy of Engineering has doubts about the feasibility of certain coal gasification processes. "Formidable engineering and operating

---

[6] Washington, D. C.: Government Printing Office, 1973.

[7] The Senate study does discuss energy prices and costs of R&D-stimulated supplies but gives no evidence as to whether the energy prices assumed clear the market, or yield surpluses, or yield shortages.

problems must be solved" and "a high element of risk is involved."[8] But we will assume that everything the bill anticipates doing can be done, and at a cost no greater than that envisioned in the Senate study. This is a generous assumption in favor of the bill, but a critic of the bill can afford to be generous.

Insofar as policy choice is to be based on the policy's consequences for people—as opposed to gaps—much more than the technical feasibility of production must be considered. We must consider first what would happen if we did not assume a shortage policy. At higher prices supply and demand would tend to equate. In this case any production of fuel from newly developed processes would have to sell at a price sufficiently low to cause consumers to shift away from other fuels. This would cause a fall in fuel prices, a clear benefit to the consumer whether he consumes the old or the newly developed energy sources. On the cost side, however, the taxpayer will have to pay the costs of the R&D (unless it is passed on as part of the consumer price of the new sources). This cost must be weighed against the consumer benefit, particular attention being paid to the fact that the costs will be paid long before the benefits are received. There will, of course, be other beneficiaries. There will be a greater demand for the talents of certain scientists and engineers and for certain kinds of government bureaucrats to run the new programs. These people will find their influence and their incomes enhanced. There are also injured parties other than the taxpayer. The wealth of those who own shares in the energy companies whose products are displaced will decline, and employees of these companies will experience a drop in the demand for their services.

To deal with some specific numbers, let us focus on the case of coal gasification R&D, a project that looms large in both S. 1283 and recent presidential energy messages. If successful, and this is not a certainty, coal gasification R&D would offer us synthetic gas at a cost of roughly $1.20-$1.60 per thousand cubic feet (mcf) at the plant.[9] (There is almost an inevitability about these matters that

---

[8] *Evaluation of Coal Gasification Technology, Part I, Pipeline Quality Gas*, a report of the National Academy of Engineers to the Department of Interior, Washington, D. C., 1974, p. iv.

[9] The Senate study gives figures of $1.25 to $1.40 in 1977 and $1.00 to $1.15 in 1980 and thereafter (Senate Interior Committee, *Energy Research and Development Prospects and Shortages*, Table 10-2, p. 92). But a task force of the National Gas Survey suggests the possibility of much higher prices. See the *Final Report of the Supply-Technical Advisory Task Force-Synthetic Gas-Coal*, National Gas Survey, Federal Power Commission (Washington, D. C.: Government Printing Office, April 1973).

makes final costs much higher than initial estimates, but let us stick with these figures.) When would the supply of synthetic gas at $1.20 per mcf cause a reduction in consumer prices of gas? To come up with a rough answer, let us look at the studies of potentially recoverable natural gas in the United States and its likely cost. The Potential Gas Agency estimates undiscovered recoverable gas at 1,200 trillion cubic feet.[10] The U.S. Geological Survey estimates the figure to be 2,100 trillion cubic feet.[11] To be conservative, we will focus on the smaller number. A separate study by Ralph Garrett of Exxon Corporation[12] estimates that this 1,200 trillion cubic feet of gas could be recovered at a cost of seventy cents per mcf or less. This is consistent with Paul MacAvoy's estimate of a 1980 market-clearing price of sixty-five cents per mcf.[13]

But the Potential Gas Agency estimate does not include gas which may be available below 30,000 feet inland and 1,500 feet of water offshore. Presumably there are large quantities of natural gas available in these regions at costs lower than $1.20 per mcf. Furthermore, with technical progress in finding and producing natural gas, costs should fall in coming decades.

Even if we exclude these potential resources at prices between seventy cents and $1.20 per mcf, we are left with over fifty years' supply of natural gas at current rates of consumption. It is true that the demand for gas will tend to grow, but remember that current demand reflects the extremely low prices set by the FPC. The average 1972 price at the wellhead was 18.4 cents per mcf, a little more than a fourth of the estimated free-market competitive price. If the wellhead price ever rises to $1.20 per mcf, the minimum break-even point for synthetic gas from coal, a substantial reduction in demand can be safely assumed.

As suggested earlier, we have little idea of energy costs and prices even twenty years from now. There is no reason to spend billions on applied research to develop supplies that may or may not

---

[10] Potential Gas Agency, Minerals Resources Institute, Colorado School of Mines, *Potential Supply of Natural Gas in the United States*, October 1971. (The latest report, just issued in December 1973 but not yet seen by the author, gives 1,146 trillion cubic feet.)

[11] U.S. Geological Survey, Circular 650. A more recent publication, "U.S. Mineral Resources," Professional Paper 820, states that the range of estimates is between 1,178 and 6,600 trillion cubic feet.

[12] "The Effect of Prices on Future Natural Gas Supplies," a paper delivered to the Potential Gas Agency meeting, Colorado Springs, 28 October 1970. This paper, representing a large research effort, has not received the attention it deserves.

[13] See MacAvoy and Pindyck, "Alternative Regulatory Policies," p. 489.

be demanded half a century from now. The only sure beneficiaries of federal coal gasification research would be the bureaucrats, politicians, scientists, and engineers associated with the research program.

Another specific example of the gap-filling approach is the plan of the Michigan-Wisconsin Pipeline Company of Detroit and the People's Natural Gas Company of Chicago to convert North Dakota coal to synthetic gas and transport it to Michigan consumers. The delivered cost of the gas in Michigan would be $1.75 per thousand cubic feet, "or roughly three and one-half times the current cost of gas in the state to the companies."[14] Unquestionably there is a gap between supply and demand for gas in Michigan. But the gap is at a price less than a third of the cost of the gas to be delivered.

Is there a gap to be filled at a price three and a half times current prices? Almost certainly not. Then how can the project succeed? Simply because the high-priced synthetic gas will be "rolled-in" with the cheap natural gas and a moderate average price will result.

But why do the pipelines want the project? Because it will increase the rate base and thus the profits of the companies, something that does not happen when higher natural gas prices are passed on to the consumer.

But why do regulatory authorities permit this to happen? Because they are basically gap-fillers and do not understand the economics of energy markets.

The coal gasification case is just one example. The Atomic Energy Commission's nuclear breeder reactor program could be cited as another dubious case. Billions have already been spent on the project, but a recent study concludes "it is *impossible* now to demonstrate a definitive *economic* advantage to society from breeder introduction,"[15] a conclusion shared by earlier Office of Management and Budget studies.

This is not to condemn all energy R&D programs. (For example, further research on oil shale would appear promising. But it is doubtful whether the government should do it.) The purpose of these remarks is to issue a warning about energy programs intended to fill gaps rather than to generate benefits in excess of costs. The original endorsement of accelerated coal gasification R&D in the President's June 1971 energy message had no basis in cost-benefit analysis. Indeed no serious attempt was made by its supporters to

---

[14] *New York Times*, 23 December 1973.

[15] I. Bupp and J. Derian, "Another Look at the Economics of the Breeder Reactor," mimeographed, November 1973, p. 18. Italics in original.

3

THE OIL MARKET:
FROM SURPLUS POLICY
TO SHORTAGE POLICY

Uses and Sources

Crude oil can be burned directly just as it comes from the ground, but it is more economical to refine it into a number of products, each suited to particular uses. In the United States gasoline is by far the largest component of refined product consumption, accounting for 49 percent by volume of 1968 total domestic consumption. In the same year, distillate fuel oil, which is used primarily for home heating, accounted for 21 percent; heavy fuel oil, which is used by electric power plants, industry, and larger commercial and residential buildings, represented another 7 percent; and jet fuel took up 3 percent. Other products included liquified gases (such as propane), kerosene, lubricating oils, asphalt, and coke. Almost 4 percent was used as feedstock to petrochemical plants.[1] This non-energy, raw material use results in products ranging from plastics, synthetic rubber, and textiles to detergents, insecticides, and fertilizers.

Another way of looking at oil product consumption is to examine the sectors of the economy that use oil. Taking 1968 again, we can see from Table 4 that the transportation sector used more than half of all oil consumed, while the industrial and residential and commercial sectors each represented less than one-fourth of the total. Consumption by electrical utilities was minor, although more recent data show it growing rapidly.

Oil competes directly with natural gas in the home heating market and with coal and natural gas in the "boiler-fuel" portions of the commercial, industrial and electric utility market. Any of these fuels can be used to provide space heating or steam for industrial

---

[1] American Petroleum Institute, *Petroleum Facts and Figures*, 1971 ed., p. 156.

Table 4

SHARES OF TOTAL PETROLEUM PRODUCTS CONSUMPTION, 1968

Energy Market	Share
Residential and commercial	24%
Industrial	17
Transportation	54
Utilities	4
Miscellaneous and unaccounted for	1
Total	100%

Source: Stanford Research Institute, "Pattern of Energy Consumption in the United States," mimeographed, November 1971, Appendix B, p. 14.

processes or for the generation of electricity. The boiler-fuel market, in which oil has at least one competitor, accounts for only about 35 percent of total oil product consumption. There are no close substitutes for the remaining 65 percent, primarily gasoline, jet fuel, and petrochemical feedstocks.[2] In this respect oil differs from coal and natural gas which compete with other fuels in virtually every market.

This division of the oil market into competing and noncompeting segments has been of some significance for public policy. In 1959 a mandatory oil import program was instituted that placed strict quantitative limitations on the importation of crude oil and oil products. By 1966, however, one product, heavy fuel oil, was admitted freely (although only along the East Coast). In view of the fact that this product competes with natural gas and coal in almost all its markets, it was one of the least important products to the industry and, therefore, the likeliest candidate for exemption from quotas. In fact, in earlier political struggles, it was the domestic coal industry that fought hardest for quotas on heavy fuel oil—the oil industry was relatively passive.[3] In 1972 heavy fuel oil represented 89 percent of all petroleum product imports and 46 percent of all oil and oil product imports, including crude.

The major source of crude oil used in the United States is, of course, domestic production, but imports have grown rapidly in the past few years. In 1959, when mandatory import quotas were

[2] We are including natural gas liquids under the heading of "oil" or "liquid petroleum." These are commonly used as petrochemical feedstocks.

[3] See Raymond Bauer, Ithiel D. Pool, and N. C. Dexter, *American Business and Public Policy*, 2d ed. (Chicago: Aldine, 1972), pp. 363-372.

established, imports represented 19 percent of domestic consumption. By 1968 this had risen to just 22 percent. Only four years later 29 percent was imported.[4]

This pattern of relative stability then sudden growth in the share of imports has little to do with the relative scarcities of domestic and foreign oil. Rather it is the outcome of shifts in public policy from surplus toward shortage worked out through the institutions of import quotas and producing-state production controls during the late 1960s.

Market-Demand Prorationing

Oil is found in underground pools or reservoirs. Property rights to mineral resources are defined in terms of boundaries projected downward from the surface. Commonly, numerous property owners hold mineral rights over a single pool. Oil is mobile underground, and raising oil to the surface in one place tends to draw it from other parts of the pool. The effective law with regard to property rights to oil is the rule of capture. Prior to the 1930s holders of the mineral rights were permitted to take as much oil as they could get by drilling on their surface property, whether or not they drew oil from under other properties. This led to competitive drilling, with each party attempting to get as much of the common pool as he could before the others got it.

Now it happens that rates of production beyond certain levels lead to lower ultimate recovery of oil. Thus, more oil could be recovered if the co-owners of the pool cooperated and produced the pool at a more moderate rate. Obviously this would be in the self-interest of the co-owners. Voluntary agreement could be reached that the pool would be operated efficiently as one unit with each co-owner receiving a share of what would have to be a larger total quantity of oil. But clearly there will tend to be considerable disagreement over what the shares should be, smaller owners frequently holding out for larger shares. In other words, the bargaining costs involved in voluntarily "unitizing" a field could be high.

In the 1930s several large discoveries were made, such as the Oklahoma City and East Texas oil fields, and large quantities of oil began to be produced, apparently in competition, as described above. Oil prices fell precipitously. Whether or not voluntary unitization would have resolved this problem eventually we shall never know

---

[4] U.S. Bureau of Mines, *Crude Petroleum, Petroleum Products, and Gas Liquids,* annual and December 1972 issues.

because state agencies stepped in and imposed mandatory prorating systems that allocated production among resource owners.[5] In some cases, besides assigning shares to resource owners, these agencies established a system for controlling the total production level for the state.[6] Thus, market-demand prorationing, as it is now called, consists of two separate aspects: an allocation of production among holders of common property—prorationing proper—and the restriction of total production to the market demand for oil at some particular price. The former aspect serves the purpose of conservation by eliminating the waste associated with competitive production from a common pool. The latter aspect is a mechanism for controlling market prices.

It is not usually recognized that the market-demand aspect of prorationing is a necessary consequence of prorationing itself. If allowable production were always set at the "maximum efficient rate of production," or MER, every producer would choose to produce at that rate. If one producer did not he would lose part of his share of the pool to other producers. Thus, even if prices fell to absurdly low levels, production at MER would continue. This is not what would happen with unitized fields. If prices fell below the expected long-run level, output from the unitized field could be cut back below MER and held in inventory for periods of higher prices. This response would be socially desirable in that production would be stimulated during periods of scarcity and inventories accumulated during periods of abundance. Prorationing continuously at MER would not have this feature and would result in a socially inefficient time pattern of production and consumption. However, the power to reduce allowables below MER so as to smooth out price fluctuations can also be used to keep prices above the levels that would exist if all fields were unitized. And it was.

---

[5] Some states have statutes permitting compulsory unitization of a field by the regulatory commission. This would be a far more efficient alternative than prorating. While Oklahoma and Louisiana now authorize compulsory unitization, it remains a controversial political issue in Texas.

[6] Major producing states with statutes authorizing the limitation of production to market demand are Kansas, New Mexico, Louisiana, Oklahoma, and Texas. Wyoming and California are the only states with production in excess of 100,000 barrels per day and do not have a "market demand" statute. But California authorizes a committee of private oil companies to carry out prorationing with similar results. See Interstate Oil Compact Commission, *A Study of Conservation of Oil and Gas* (Oklahoma City, 1964). For an extensive discussion of prorationing by an economist, see Stephen MacDonald, *Petroleum Conservation in the United States* (Baltimore: The Johns Hopkins University Press, 1971).

The rationale for prorationing has been presented so well by William J. Murray, Jr., a former chairman of the Texas Railroad Commission (TRC), that the reader deserves his exposition:

Assume a return to the date of the unfenced, open range. Also assume the absence of cattle brands and that the "rule of capture" which the courts have applied to the oil industry was applicable to ranching. Each rancher would turn his cattle loose on the range and would recover from the open range not that number which had initially belonged to him but the number which he could capture, slaughter and sell. Human nature being what it is, each rancher would be forced to immediately round up and slaughter all the cattle he could, selling meat anywhere he could for any price he could get. For a time the consumers would rejoice over the surplus supply of beef at amazingly low prices. They would eat T-bone steak three meals a day and fill their refrigerators and deep freezes, but there would be a limit to the amount that could be eaten and stored and soon appalling waste comparable to the destruction of the buffalo herds in earlier years would take place. After the cattle had been slaughtered and wasted, supplies of beef would dwindle, stores from the deep freezes would be exhausted, and then the price for the inadequate remaining supply of cattle would soar. The consumer would discover that his brief period of feasting on absurdly cheap meat would result in a long period of fasting on outrageously high and scarce supplies of meat.

If these assumed conditions existed it would be necessary both for the protection of the consumer and the producers of beef that some governmental authority prorate to each rancher his rightful share of the community supply and that the total quantity allocated daily or monthly to the various ranchers be only that quantity which the public would consume. It is, of course, readily acknowledged that the demand for beef is not an absolute quantity, but that it does vary to some extent with price. It would be the task of the regulatory authority to allocate the quantity of beef to be slaughtered so as to assure the consuming public of a constant dependable supply with adequate reserves for the future and at the cheapest possible price, but the cheapest average price would not be obtained by temporary, wasteful surpluses which would depress prices followed by soaring prices from consequent scarcities.

Thus it is with oil. Without proration by a state regulatory authority, each producer is legally entitled to all the oil he can capture and sell from a common oil reservoir. There are no fences underground. It is always open range and the law of capture applies as far as the oil man is concerned. Without proration a wasteful flood of oil would recur as in the early life of the East Texas Field.[7]

The upshot of this is that from the 1930s to at least 1970—but definitely not since April 1973—the U.S. crude oil producing market was not free. It was cartelized. A cartel exists when there are either restrictions on who can sell in a market or on how much anyone can sell. Oil production under market-demand prorationing was cartelized because producers' output was restricted by regulatory commissions. Entry into the industry as a seller was and is unrestricted.

Most of us are familiar with a number of cartels or closed markets. Physicians, lawyers, public accountants, pharmacists, and taxicab operators are members of cartels because not just anyone can offer their services in these fields. Before setting up shop in any of these industries, one must acquire a license, usually issued by a state commission or board. Farmers are members of cartels not because entry into farming is restricted but because acreage controls limit production. Physicians justify their cartel by pointing out the higher standards of medicine brought about by licensing. Oil men justify their cartel by citing the greater conservation of oil. Both are unquestionably correct—the levels of medicine and conservation are higher. However, in addition, prices of both medical services and oil are higher because their supply is restricted. Thus, there was nothing unusual or devious about the domestic petroleum cartel. It was established by state laws, endorsed by federal law (the Connally Hot Oil Act), and even operated in Texas by officials elected in statewide voting. Like many cartels, it was the outcome of a highly democratic process.

How were prices and overall market supplies determined in this cartel? With regard to price, it appears that some large purchaser of crude (also a seller) would change his purchasing price. If a sufficiently large number of other purchasers followed suit, the new price would stick. If not, the price change would be cancelled. In this way, when large-volume crude purchasers wanted a different price, that price would be realized.

---

[7] "Market Demand Proration," in U.S. Congress, Senate, Committee on the Judiciary, *Governmental Intervention in the Market Mechanism: The Petroleum Industry*, Hearings before the Subcommittee on Antitrust and Monopoly, 91st Congress, 1st session (1969), Part 2, "Industry View," pp. 1070-1071.

In general, high-cost producers prefer prices higher than those preferred by low-cost producers. Thus, any actual price in the market would not reflect everyone's idea of what the optimal or profit-maximizing price is. Precisely how the opinions of different firms were weighted is unclear. All we know for certain is that the price prevailing in the crude oil market (before government price controls) was lower than some firms wanted and higher than other firms wanted.

But the price-setting process used by a cartel is not nearly so crucial to its survival as the system that controls production. Much of the success of the domestic crude oil cartel is owed to the procedure used for setting production levels. Again, no one has described it so well as William Murray:

> In regard to the Railroad Commission of Texas, the Attorney General reported that for seven of the eleven years under study Texas annual production was never as much as one percent above or below actual demand and that for the five year period from 1952 through 1956 the weighted average for Texas production missed the actual demand by only 11/100 of one percent.
>
> Following this revelation of amazing accuracy in balancing supply to demand, the skeptic finally inquires as to how the Texas Railroad Commission is able to do it. To better enable it to estimate future demand, the Commission is constantly making forecasts of all types, but it must be acknowledged that the Commissioners are not the economic wizards or the crystal ball gazers that they are sometimes credited with being. There is actually a relatively simple method for determining market demand. This method is sometimes compared with that used by the city of Austin to determine the demand for water. Water is pumped out of the city lake into a reservoir on top of a hill from whence it flows to the consumers. If too much water is pumped into this reservoir it will overflow and be wasted; if too little is pumped there will be inadequate pressure on the mains and some of the consumers will not have all of the supply they need. However, it is not necessary to accurately forecast the total demand for water on a hot summer day. Instead it is only necessary to observe the level of water stored in the reservoir. From experience those operating the pump at the lake know at what level the reservoir should be maintained. If water is below the proper level and is declining, then the consumers are using more than is being pumped and it is necessary to speed up the pumps. If the

water is above the proper level and is rising, then the pumps must be retarded else waste will occur.

This is essentially the method followed by the Railroad Commission. At periodic hearings the proper levels of crude oil stocks and products for the nation are determined. If crude oil and product stocks are above the proper levels and are increasing, then it requires no crystal ball to determine that production in excess of market demand is occurring and that if waste is to be avoided a reduction in allowables must be ordered.

On the other hand if stocks of crude oil and products are below the proper levels and are declining then an increase in allowables is desired in order to bring supply and demand in balance.

Once each month the Railroad Commission holds a hearing to determine the number of producing days to be set for the following month. Testimony is received from all interested parties, many factors are considered, but the primary determining factor is whether the above ground stocks of crude and four principal products are in excess or below the proper level.[8]

It is sometimes thought that the success of market-demand prorationing depended heavily upon monthly petroleum demand forecasts issued by the Bureau of Mines prior to the monthly TRC hearings.[9] Mr. Murray's statement belies the importance of this, as do TRC procedures. Furthermore, a 1971 White House directive, issued when allowables were still below 100 percent, delayed the release of the Bureau of Mines forecasts until after each monthly hearing with no perceptible effect on the TRC, the hearings, or the allowables set.

It must be stressed that the TRC and other state commissions did not set prices—they ratified prices set by refiner-purchasers by tailoring production to just meet demand at those prices.[10]

The surplus capacity generated by market-demand prorationing can be calculated from estimates of productive capacity and actual production data. The only source of productive capacity estimates on a state-by-state basis are those of the Independent Petroleum Asso-

---

8 Ibid., pp. 1071-1072.

9 For example, this is the view of M. Mann in his testimony before the Senate Special Subcommittee on Integrated Oil Operations, 28 November 1973, p. 444 of the transcript.

10 Professor Adelman holds the view that on at least one occasion the TRC used its production allowables to force a price increase. See Adelman, World Petroleum Market, pp. 151-158.

ciation of America.[11] The association's estimates indicate that in 1965 Texas could have increased production from non-stripper wells by 84 percent, Louisiana, 62 percent, Kansas, 30 percent, California, 16 percent, and New Mexico, 10 percent.[12] The association estimated total U.S. productive capacity for all wells to be 3.7 billion barrels in the same year. Actual production was 2.7 billion barrels, indicating a surplus capacity of more than 25 percent. This is not to suggest that under a policy of compulsory unitization productive capacity would have been fully utilized. Some voluntarily held spare capacity would exist under compulsory unitization, but it certainly would be less than 25 percent.

How well did the domestic petroleum cartel do? The measure of cartel effectiveness is profits earned, which depend upon the proximity of cartel price to profit-maximizing price and actual costs to minimum costs. On the price side it is clear that the domestic cartel price was substantially above the price that would have existed in a competitive market with unitized fields (and substantially above the delivered foreign price when imports became a factor). How close the domestic cartel price was to the optimal price is hard to say.

What *is* obvious is that the costs of production under the government-operated cartel were enormously higher than they would have been under an efficient cartel or competition. The formula for allocating production shares among producers was extremely generous to small high-cost producers and extremely stingy to low-cost producers. Wells producing less than twenty barrels per day—so called "stripper wells"—were usually exempted from regulation entirely. Furthermore, there was no barrier erected to prevent new high-cost producers from entering the market, thereby forcing cutbacks in low-cost production and further raising costs. The result was a "system of organized waste" that would be difficult to parallel. Adelman's estimate of *added* costs over the competitive market in 1961 is eighty cents to one dollar per barrel or 40-50 percent of the delivered price of foreign crude.[13] By and large these excess costs were imposed on major oil companies and larger producers.

It is certain that numerous inefficient producers were enriched by the cartel. Tens of thousands of stripper wells owed their survival to

---

[11] "Report of Productive Capacity Committee," mimeographed, May 1968.

[12] See statement of Dr. Henry Steele in U.S. Congress, Senate, Committee on the Judiciary, *Governmental Intervention in the Market Mechanism: The Petroleum Industry*, Part 1, "Economists View," pp. 208-233.

[13] M. A. Adelman, "Efficiency of Resource Use in Crude Petroleum," *Southern Economic Journal*, October 1964, pp. 101-122.

it. The profits of medium-sized and larger producers, however, appear to be substantially below the normal rate of return earned by U.S. industry during the past two decades. For these firms the added costs seem to have more than offset the higher prices.[14]

It should be stressed that this cartel was operated by the government and could *only* have been operated by the government. The structure of the crude oil producing industry was and is sufficiently competitive to make a private cartel impossible. Indeed, the major companies would never have designed a system so overwhelmingly hostile to their interests. The production control systems developed appear to be the work of small producers employing their relatively greater influence on state legislatures, another example of the tyranny of the small over the large familiar to students of political economy.

In April 1972, due primarily to changes in U.S. oil import policy which will be elaborated below, production allowables rose to 100 percent of the maximum efficient rate. Market-demand prorationing is no longer restricting crude oil production. But circumstances in the world market and shifts in import policy could easily change and again make market-demand prorationing an effective device for supporting artificially high petroleum prices, stimulating high-cost production, and raising the costs of more efficient producers. The institution of compulsory unitization and the abolition of market-demand prorationing would assure more efficient exploitation of petroleum resources in the future.

Oil Imports: A Brief History [15]

As late as 1946 the United States was shipping more oil overseas than it was receiving. But this positive balance was never realized again as exports fell from their modest wartime levels, while imports rose for more than a decade without interruption. By 1955 overseas imports had increased four times, and domestic producers were concerned that the substantial post-war price increases—in 1955 crude oil was selling at more than twice its wartime level—would be washed out by the foreign onslaught and that domestic production would have to be cut back to make room for the indefinite expansion of overseas imports.

The source of these rapidly growing imports was the burgeoning low-cost production of the Middle East and Venezuela. This pro-

---

[14] See my testimony before the Senate Interior Committee, Appendix B.

[15] This section draws freely upon my paper, "U.S. Oil Import Policy," *Business Economics*, January 1974.

duction potential seemed—and was—almost unlimited compared to the size of the market. From 1950 to 1957 the major Middle East producing nations—Iran, Iraq, Kuwait, and Saudi Arabia—more than doubled production, and there was far more oil just waiting for a drill bit. This potential is exemplified by the tenfold increase in Saudi Arabian production since 1950—and that country's production limit is nowhere in sight.

For U.S. producers there was no remedy for these bleak prospects in the private sector. The only recourse was political: join the trek to Washington and seek relief from an institution capable of applying coercion—the federal government. Initially, however, the federal response was not coercive. A voluntary import program was set up in the hope that importers would recognize their overall long-term interests—most importers were also domestic producers—and cooperate by limiting imports. At first an informal arrangement was set up. In 1957, as new firms continued to enter the import business, this informal approach was displaced by a more serious, but still voluntary, regulatory effort. The "newcomers" also undermined the second voluntary program, some small companies raising imports rapidly to take advantage of a fifty to sixty cent per barrel, or 20 percent, differential between delivered domestic and overseas crude. As a result, overseas imports rose almost 40 percent over the four-year life of the voluntary programs.

In March 1959 the Mandatory Oil Import Program went into effect. It continued until April 1973. The mechanism chosen to restrict imports was a quota fixed as a percentage of domestic production. Obviously there were many possible alternatives: a quota fixed in absolute amount, a fixed tariff, or a tariff varying with the level of imports. Given that a quota was chosen, there was still the choice of how to allocate import licenses. They could have been auctioned to the highest bidders. Instead they were mainly allocated to refiners on the basis of refinery inputs. Economic analysis suggests that, of the alternatives, this system assured the highest domestic crude oil prices given the proportion of imports to domestic consumption.[16]

The allocation of import licenses among refiners was not in proportion to refinery inputs. Small refiners were given a disproportionately large share. For example, in 1969 a 10,000-barrel-per-day refiner received licenses to import 1,950 barrels per day, or 19.5 percent, while a 500,000-barrel-per-day refiner received licenses to import 21,050 barrels per day, or 4.2 percent. With import licenses worth

---

[16] E. Mitchell, R. Tollison, and E. Tower, "Tariffs versus Quotas to Control Oil Imports," mimeographed, November 1972.

$1.25 per barrel, this meant per-barrel subsidies of 24.4 cents to the small refiner and 5.3 cents to the large refiner. Uniform subsidies tend to be competed through to consumers while special subsidies do not. Much of the value of import licenses went to support inefficient operations or, in the short run, into the pockets of small refiners as excess profit.

If we are to judge the quota program by the extent to which it restricted imports, it would have to be judged a success, at least up until 1967. Overseas imports rose 27 percent in the first eight years of the program. Domestic production rose 29 percent, putting overseas imports in a slightly poorer relative position. Furthermore, almost two-thirds of the increment in imports was in the form of heavy fuel oil, which is highly competitive with domestic natural gas and coal, and on which domestic refineries had been cutting back yields for three decades.

Looking at the main target of the mandatory quotas, the domestic price of crude oil, the program must also be judged a success—again, up until the past few years. In spite of considerable excess capacity in the domestic producing industry, U.S. crude prices remained virtually constant through the 1960s, typically running $1.25 per barrel (or 60 percent) over the landed foreign cost.

The costs of the quota program have been assessed in several studies.[17] Estimates of added consumer costs of oil products run around $6 billion for 1969. Resources used unnecessarily in the domestic production of oil that could have been purchased at a lower cost abroad have been valued at $500 million to $1 billion per year. No estimates have been made of the costs of inefficient refinery capacity kept in existence by an import license allocation program that was, in effect, a subsidy to small refiners.

By the late 1960s it became clear that either the domestic price or the proportion of imports would have to be allowed to rise significantly. Additions to domestic reserves at the prevailing prices were insufficient to maintain the historical degree of U.S. self-sufficiency. Texas allowables were rising during the late 1960s. Production at 100 percent was just down the road. Left alone, under the protection of the import quota, prices would have risen substantially. Instead, operating under the constraints of a very different political environment—Johnson, Rayburn, and Kerr were gone—and an atmosphere of

---

[17] See J. Burrows and T. Domencich, *An Analysis of the United States Oil Import Quota* (Lexington, Mass.: Lexington Books, 1970), and Cabinet Task Force on Oil Import Control, *The Oil Import Question* (Washington, D. C.: Government Printing Office, 1970).

concern about inflation, the industry was able to gain only two twenty-five-cent-per-barrel increases, one in February 1969 and the other in November 1970. At the end of 1972 real U.S. crude prices (deflated by the wholesale price index) stood 5 percent *below* their 1967 level.

Quotas have been continuously expanded in recent years to keep the real domestic price down by meeting rising domestic demand through imports. Crude imports had been fixed as a percentage of domestic production in the 1960s. After 1970, they were allowed to fill the projected gap between domestic crude supply and total domestic demand at current prices. This meant sharply rising imports with domestic production peaking in 1970. In the two years following the decision to set quotas on a "gap" basis (1971-72), imports rose almost 40 percent.

Setting the quotas at the difference between domestic demand and domestic production at available capacity meant that control over price passed from the producing states and industry to the federal government. And federal policy aimed at keeping nominal or money prices relatively stable. Prices were neither as high as the industry would have liked, nor as low as they would have been with no quotas or larger quotas.

In the spring of 1973, due to a combination of higher f.o.b. foreign crude prices and higher tanker rates, the price of delivered foreign crude rose to levels comparable to domestic crude. In these circumstances the quotas served no function except to allocate the foreign crude among importers. The quotas were not keeping oil out, nor were they keeping domestic prices up. Even as allocators of the right to import they were no longer allocating anything of value because the spread between domestic and foreign prices had disappeared.

With the inevitability of shortages in gasoline and heating oil (if economy-wide price controls continued), the quota program became a curious anomaly, virtually without reasonable defense. In April 1973 the President announced the end of import quotas and their replacement by a system of license fees—a euphemism for tariffs—on crude and petroleum products. Thus the surplus policy that had dominated the U.S. oil market for almost three decades came to an end.

The New Oil Import Program

On 18 April 1973, the President signed the proclamation that removed mandatory quotas on crude oil and oil product imports and substituted a system of license fees to encourage domestic production and refining. The schedule of fees sets different rates for crude, gasoline, and the other covered products, and all the fees are to rise gradually, reaching their maximums in November 1975. The per-barrel fees are: 10.5 cents rising to twenty-one cents for crude, fifty-two cents rising to sixty-three cents for gasoline, and fifteen cents rising to sixty-three cents on the other covered products. No fees were imposed on ethane, propane, butane, and asphalt imports.

The higher fees on gasoline and other products as compared to crude are intended to encourage the construction of domestic refineries. The differential of forty-two cents per barrel (sixty-three cents minus twenty-one cents) between product and crude license fees after November 1975 is the measure of protection given to existing domestic refineries by the fee schedule. In addition, new refineries will receive 75 percent of their crude imports fee-exempt for the first five years. Thus, the total protection for new refineries is forty-two cents plus 15.75 cents (twenty-one cents times .75), or 57.25 cents for the first five years of operation. Protection and encouragement of domestic crude production is measured simply by the twenty-one-cent crude license fee.

Under the old quota program licenses were subject only to a 10.5-cent-per-barrel tariff imposed by Congress, but the quantities imported by each firm were restricted by the quota allocation. The new program drops this tariff and replaces it with new, higher license fees, but it also excludes from fees classes of importers that had held quotas under the old program. These fee-exempt licenses accounted for the overwhelming bulk of imports in 1973. In subsequent years the quantity of fee-exempt tickets will be reduced by formula, and by 1980 all imports will be fee-paying.

The major groups of importers and the quantity of fee-exempt tickets they received in 1973 were:

Refiners and petrochemical plants east of the Rockies: 1,992,000 barrels of crude and unfinished oils per day.

Refiners and petrochemical plants west of the Rockies: 670,000 barrels of crude and unfinished oils per day.

Importers of heavy fuel oil along the East Coast: 2,900,000 barrels per day.

Importers of heavy fuel oil west of the Rockies: 75,600 barrels per day.

Remaining importers of heavy fuel oil: 42,000 barrels per day.

Refiners of Canadian crude oil east of the Rockies: 960,000 barrels per day.

Refiners of Canadian crude oil west of the Rockies: 280,000 barrels per day.

Deepwater terminal operators on the East Coast: 50,000 barrels per day.

In addition, the Oil Import Appeals Board is empowered until 1980 to grant additional fee-exempt product tickets "in emergencies" or to firms experiencing "exceptional hardship."

A little more than two months after the announcement of the new program another presidential proclamation was signed. It modified the treatment of Canadian product imports refined from Canadian crude. Under the provisions of the proclamation, fees on these imports were postponed until May 1974, and will increase more slowly than those on other product imports, not reaching sixty-three cents per barrel until November 1980.

Two major economic issues are raised by the new program: (1) How do the levels of protection granted to domestic refiners and producers by the license-fee system relate to national security or reliability considerations, and (2) will windfall profits be realized under the program, and, if so, to whom will they accrue? The protection offered to a new domestic refinery is 57.75 cents per barrel for the first five years and forty-two cents per barrel for the remaining life of the refinery. The value added by a new foreign refinery would be about $1.20 per barrel. Thus, the protection offered runs close to 50 percent of the value produced for the first five years and 35 percent thereafter. These are high rates of protection by U.S. tariff standards. As a point of reference, consider the fact that in 1970 the Cabinet Task Force on Oil Import Control recommended a ten-cent-per-barrel, or less than 10 percent, level of protection.

The protection offered by the new license fee or tariff schedule would seem to be more than necessary to assure a high degree of domestic refining self-sufficiency. The cost advantages of the cheapest alternative—a Caribbean refinery—depend, of course, on many factors, including tax treatment by the foreign government concerned, the rate of return required on an inherently riskier investment, and the existence of U.S. East Coast superports. But even assuming no East Coast superports, zero taxes, and no risk premium on foreign Caribbean refineries, we arrive at a cost differential of only thirty-four cents per barrel.[18] A firm would most likely want to earn a higher rate of return to offset the risks of foreign operations, or to locate in

---

[18] These calculations are based on the National Petroleum Council's *Factors Affecting U.S. Petroleum Refining* (Washington, D. C., May 1973). They assume a "balanced" refinery as opposed to the type built recently in the U.S. which minimizes heavy products. The calculations also assume a discounted cash flow rate of return of 10 percent.

the U.S. Virgin Islands (which would involve higher taxes). Either of these alternatives would tend to lower the differential to between twenty and twenty-five cents, depending upon the particular tax arrangements or return premium. Thus, protection on the order of twenty-five to thirty cents per barrel would appear to be adequate to assure construction of refineries in the U.S., with a possible exception here and there due to some uniquely attractive foreign situation.

But how badly should we want a very high degree of domestic refining self-sufficiency? The concern about refineries in the past fifteen years has been that they were almost all being built outside the U.S. If that trend continued a question of national security might arise. It is doubtful, however, that national security requires that *all* new refineries built to supply the U.S. market be located in the U.S. Foreign refinery capacity is scattered over many nations. No one nation would supply an appreciable percentage of U.S. consumption, nor is it likely that any group of nations would conspire to cut off refined products to the U.S. The national security aspect of refining is very different from that of crude supply. A more modest degree of protection—twenty-five to thirty cents per barrel for all refineries [19]— would probably assure a high degree of security and at the same time enable some foreign refineries to compete in the U.S. market, providing independent marketers with wider sources of supply.

The protection offered to domestic producers will be twenty-one cents per barrel in 1975. This is about 3 percent of the current value of domestic or foreign crude. (The Cabinet Task Force recommended a $1.35 per barrel tariff. This was the normal differential between domestic and foreign crude prices under the old quota program of the 1960s.)

How much additional domestic production does this twenty-one-cent fee or tariff buy and how much imported crude oil will be displaced? The answer depends upon the long-term elasticity of supply of domestic crude with respect to price. A reasonable range of elasticities would be 0.5 to 1.0. This means a 1 percent differential in domestic price would result in a one-half to 1 percent increase in domestic supply. If we were producing 11 million barrels per day in 1980 without this twenty-one-cent tariff, production could jump to 11.3 to 11.6 million barrels per day with the tariff. If we were importing 10 million barrels per day in 1980, this would fall to 9.4 to 9.7 million barrels per day. Obviously, a tariff of twenty-one cents per barrel on

---

[19] The purpose of a subsidy to domestic refining is not only to get new refineries built, but also to keep old refineries in existence. Economic efficiency would suggest the same subsidy to old and new refineries.

crude oil makes little difference in the U.S. import picture or in its reliance on Middle East crude oil.

With recent sharp increases in world crude prices the United States can be expected to become far more self-sufficient—providing that domestic crude is permitted to sell at free-market prices. Still it takes considerable time for the industry to bring new crude sources on stream. The normal lag from initial exploration and discovery to the consumer is three to five years, and sparsely explored and distant areas, such as Alaska, will take longer than that. Furthermore, there will be the inevitable delays brought about by environmental suits and the normal sluggishness of government in setting up leasing programs on federal lands. Therefore, we must be prepared to import oil in large quantities for an interim period, particularly from the Middle East and North Africa.

Should a special government program, such as oil stockpiling, be created as a precaution against future cutoffs of imported oil? In a truly free domestic oil market such a program would be unnecessary. Businessmen face the problem of unreliable supplies every day and solve it by maintaining a diversity of sources, spare capacity, and additional inventories. They do this not because they are concerned about the hardships imposed on their customers in the event of a shortfall in supplies, but because it is expected to be profitable. When shortfalls occur, prices will rise and they will be able to profitably sell the additional inventories and produce from their spare capacity. It is the expectation of profit from exploiting these situations of unusual scarcity that makes the holding of added inventories and spare capacity worthwhile.

This approach to the reliability problem has two socially desirable consequences: first, it reduces the impact of any shortfall by providing additional supplies in times of scarcity and thereby reduces the price necessary to meet demand. Second, it reduces the likelihood of a deliberate cutoff of supplies since its impact on consumers is reduced.

For this approach to be optimal two conditions must be met: first, the suppliers in the private sector must have as much knowledge as possible about the likelihood of a cutoff. Second, the same firms must believe they will be able to profit in case future cutoffs occur—by selling at free-market prices in periods of scarcity. It is safe to assume that the first condition can be met. It is the second condition that has been and will be difficult to meet. Many do not support free-market prices during periods of unusual scarcity. The political process tends to choose shortage policies and price controls in such situations, at least for a time. Businessmen know this and therefore hold smaller inventories and less spare capacity than they would under optimal conditions.

To remedy this inadequate preparation for import cutoffs, the government could require importers to maintain extra inventories or spare capacity as a condition of importing. It is not desirable for the government to stockpile oil itself, or even to specify the manner in which importers stockpile oil. It may be cheaper for some firms to maintain spare capacity in some wells and in their transportation system than to store oil in tanks. Closing in some high-cost stripper wells and keeping them on tap for emergencies might prove economical in some cases. All the government needs to verify is that additional oil can be delivered when it is wanted. For the government to hold oil itself, or specify the method that private firms must use to hold oil, would result in unnecessary costs.

It should be noted that this suggested intervention of government is not the result of imperfections in the free market. As is commonly the case, the demand for this government action is the consequence of other government actions, actual or potential.

Product prices in the United States will be higher under the new import program as compared to prices under free trade. The price differentials will result from the following elements: higher resource costs to the nation in refining and producing, economic rents or windfalls to various segments of the industry, and revenues to the federal treasury. A detailed analysis of this breakdown is inappropriate here; however, one point is worth mentioning. Assuming that no significant amount of fee-exempt licenses will be issued by the Oil Import Appeals Board, there are likely to be windfalls to established importers of petroleum products, especially on imports of heavy fuel oil and home heating oil. Imports of these products are likely to exceed the amount of fee-exempt licenses issued in the coming years and fee-paying imports will still set the domestic price. For heavy fuel oil the value of fee-exempt licenses in 1975 will be $550 million per year if fee-paying imports are coming in that early. Without changes in the program this value will accrue to importers as a windfall.

The World Market

Until the past year events in the world oil market had only a minor influence on the U.S. market. The surplus policy adopted by federal and state governments effectively insulated the U.S. from developments abroad. The shifts after 1969 from a surplus policy to a free market and then to a shortage policy have made the actions of Middle East producers, especially Saudi Arabia, a dominant influence on the U.S. market.

The broad facts regarding the world oil market over the last two decades are not in dispute.[20] After World War II, Middle East oil sold in the U.S. market at prices competitive with domestic crude. Three trends occurred over the next twenty years. First, the concentration of production among major producing countries and major producing companies declined sharply. In 1950 Iran, Saudi Arabia, Venezuela, and Kuwait accounted for 90 percent of the production of the major foreign, free world oil-producing countries, roughly 3.1 out of 3.3 million barrels per day. By 1969, they had 12.1 out of 21.3 million barrels per day, or 55 percent. In 1950 the four leading oil companies—Exxon, BP, Shell, and Gulf—had 83 percent of the output of the major foreign, free world oil-producing countries. By 1969 their share had declined to 56 percent.

Second, the price of crude in the Persian Gulf fell substantially. In 1950 the price of Arabian crude was $1.85 f.o.b., Persian Gulf. By 1969 this price had fallen to $1.27 (or ninety-eight cents when adjusted for changes in the U.S. wholesale price index). This was still well above the typical cost of production of Middle East crude (about ten cents per barrel), but the price trend was clearly down.

Finally, a turnaround in world prices began in 1970. By the fall of 1973 Persian Gulf prices had far surpassed controlled U.S. prices, reaching more than eight dollars per barrel by January 1974. An important device in raising the cartel price—and, thus, the world price—was the shift to per-barrel taxes. Key members of the Organization of Petroleum Exporting Countries (OPEC) had shifted to de facto per-barrel taxes by 1960 (although the taxes were still called income taxes). With adjustments for transportation and crude quality, these taxes gave the producing nations an improved mechanism for discouraging competitive production among countries by, in effect, selling licenses to produce at coordinated prices. It is generally agreed that the major oil companies were passive participants in this process.

What is in dispute is why the Persian Gulf price has turned around so sharply in the past few years. According to one view, this turnaround was inevitable because of increasing cohesiveness of the members of OPEC, the projected dominance of Saudi Arabia (and possibly Iran) in future markets, and the enormous revenues of OPEC members—particularly Saudi Arabia—relative to their domestic

---

[20] See Adelman, *World Petroleum Market*, passim.

needs.[21] According to this view, all that could be done was to make an attempt to stabilize the situation by international negotiation. Oil prices of five or ten dollars per barrel were a necessary outcome.

Another view has it that there was nothing inevitable about the turnaround in prices.[22] Rather, it was the result of incompetent U.S. State Department dealings with a highly fragile cartel. Had the U.S. not passively accepted Libyan production cutbacks in 1970, nor given what was tantamount to outright endorsement of higher prices in Teheran in 1971, the OPEC nations would have returned to the competitive pricing patterns of the past two decades and prices would have continued to fall.

Whichever view is correct, it is now obvious that the OPEC cartel has the upper hand and is fully exploiting its position.

Since September 1973, Persian Gulf export prices have risen from about $3.10 to $8.30 per barrel (as of January 1974). Perhaps the most critical aspect of future oil policy is the path of future prices. Some forecasters see still higher crude prices down the road. On the other hand, some economists, such as Professors Friedman and Houthakker, believe that current prices already exceed the level that would maximize long-run cartel profits. And one leading oil consultant, Walter Levy, sees serious problems for the cartel in maintaining current prices over the decade. Current prices, they argue, would so reduce demand and stimulate supply that cartel revenues would be smaller than if prices were cut back. The large expected response of demand and supply to changes in world crude prices is evidenced by a recent study done for the Organization for Economic Cooperation and Development which shows 1980 oil exports to North America, Western Europe, and Japan at half the level predicted before the recent sharp escalation in prices. Incidentally, most of the change in oil import demand is likely to occur in the United States since it has far better energy resource opportunities than most other OECD nations.[23]

The possibility of a decline in world crude prices is also taken very seriously by the U.S. Department of Commerce, and thus by implication, by some major U.S. energy companies since the department generally represents U.S. business interests and puts forward

---

[21] James Akins, "The Oil Crisis," *Foreign Affairs*, April 1973.

[22] M. A. Adelman, "Is the Oil Shortage Real?" *Foreign Policy*, no. 9 (Winter 1972-1973).

[23] This means that the dollar and the U.S. exchange rate will probably be favorably affected by continued high oil prices. See E. J. Mitchell and W. Eizenga, "The Oil Crisis and World Monetary Arrangements," Amsterdam-Rotterdam Bank N.V., *Economic Quarterly Review*, June 1974.

their views in the councils of government. The Commerce Department has recently offered a plan to provide a guarantee of high prices—in the same range as those prevailing now in world markets—for unconventional petroleum substitutes. There is hardly a need for a guaranteed price if one is confident prices will not fall.

Predicting the path of future oil prices requires a knowledge of world demand and supply responses to price. In addition, it requires a knowledge of precisely which nations comprise the world petroleum cartel. High cartel or monopoly prices can only be maintained if production is curtailed in the exporting nations. To the extent that an exporting nation does not curtail production, it is not a true member of a cartel in the economic sense, whatever its formal status in international organizations such as OPEC.

During the recent Arab embargo only Arab nations curtailed output. Most other exporting nations continued to expand production. Between September and November 1973 Arab producers reduced production by 23 percent, from 20.5 million barrels per day to 15.7 million barrels per day. This amounted to a reduction of 8 percent in world oil production. In January 1974 Arab production rose to 17.6 million barrels per day, and it is likely that, with the suspension of the embargo, production will return to the September 1973 levels in all Arab nations, except Libya and Kuwait, which will apparently continue their production at the January levels.

The success of the Arab producers in achieving coordinated cutbacks in production for a brief period does not imply that curtailed production can easily be achieved in the long run. And yet that is what must happen if current (or still higher) prices are to be sustained. Oil demand and supply are very insensitive to price in the short run. Over a period of years demand and supply adjustments will necessitate far smaller exports than anticipated earlier, as the OECD study suggests. This is where the question of precisely who comprises the cartel comes in. If the cartel is composed only of Arab nations, then those nations must bear the full brunt of curtailment while "free-riders," such as Iran, Venezuela, Nigeria, and Indonesia, derive full benefits. But limiting the cartel to just the Arab nations may still be too broad. Iraq, the third largest Arab producer, did not curtail production during the Arab embargo. Actually, it increased production by 5 percent from September to January. Other smaller Arab producers will find that their curtailment has little positive effect on price and considerable negative effect on their income. While this is very speculative, it could turn out in the long run that the cartel will amount to just Saudi Arabia, Kuwait, and Abu Dhabi—and perhaps just Saudi Arabia. If so, the most profitable cartel price will be much lower than for an all-OPEC or all-Arab cartel.

The actions of Saudi Arabia at the Vienna OPEC meeting in March suggest that in the long run the cartel may be rather narrowly based and that the optimal cartel price may be lower than the March 1974 price. A majority of the members of OPEC wanted to raise prices but were dissuaded when Saudi Arabia threatened to resign from the organization.[24] While this disagreement may have been due partly to noneconomic considerations, it is certainly consistent with the view that the cartel is narrowly based and that the current price is higher than the price that would maximize cartel profits. The view that "political" as opposed to "economic" considerations may dominate future cartel decisions does not really change the analysis much. Political strength is largely a function of a nation's economic status. And, furthermore, it is not easy to imagine a nation sacrificing its own economic position to achieve political gains, especially if its actions simultaneously enrich other nations at its expense and therefore endow these other nations with greater future political influence relative to its own.

What can U.S. energy policy do to reduce the price charged by the oil cartel? At first glance, one might imagine that simply reducing imports would have that effect, but this is not necessarily true. What determines whether a cartel raises or lowers its price is the elasticity of demand it faces. It is not certain that reducing U.S. imports will make remaining U.S. oil import demand more elastic. U.S. energy policy vis-à-vis the cartel should focus directly on making import demand more sensitive to price, that is, more elastic. To put it simply, if higher prices mean a large drop in oil exports for the producing countries and lower prices mean a large increase, we are more likely to get lower prices than if imports are insensitive to price.

Unfortunately, some present and contemplated policies have the opposite effect. Price controls on domestic oil mean that any increase in the imported oil price is not passed on fully to the consumer. With domestic oil supplying 60 percent of U.S. consumption, an increase of one dollar per barrel in the cartel price means only a forty-cent increase in the U.S. consumer's price. Price controls, by partially insulating the U.S. consumer from the cartel, induce the cartel to charge him a higher price. (Fortunately, most major consuming nations have not adopted this policy.) Furthermore, the lower the

---

[24] Clyde H. Farensworth, "Algerian Says Oil-Buying Nations Conspire on Price," *New York Times*, 21 March 1974, p. 37.

domestic price, the smaller will be domestic supplies—and the more high-priced foreign oil we must buy.

The recent proposal of the U.S. Department of Commerce to guarantee high prices on unconventional energy sources by means of government subsidies also would have this perverse effect. To the extent that U.S. domestic supplies are independent of the world price, there is little incentive for the cartel to lower that price.

U.S. oil policy should be founded on the premise that we will buy cheap, reliable foreign oil. This policy would make sense if we had no influence over the world price. With U.S. demand becoming a major determinant of the world price, it is doubly important to adopt this approach.

Recent Oil Policy Decisions

Throughout the 1950s and '60s, government, through the institutions of market-demand prorationing and import quotas, gave us a surplus policy toward the domestic producing industry. Excess capacity existed in domestic oil production because prices were higher than necessary to clear the market. While this policy gave consumers substantial protection against cutoffs of foreign supplies and insulated the U.S. market from the vagaries of the world market, it also placed heavy costs on U.S. consumers and wasted billions of dollars in unnecessary drilling activity. The beneficiaries of this policy were small stripper-well producers.

By 1969, uncertainty arose regarding the future of U.S. policy. At prevailing domestic crude and natural gas prices the petroleum industry could not be expected to maintain the historical relationship between domestic production and consumption. In 1969 the Cabinet Task Force on Oil Import Control was formed. It issued a report calling for a switch to a tariff system. The proposal was rejected by the President. Significantly, the President was given a choice of continued quotas or a tariff that would reduce the domestic price. The option of a tariff that would maintain the domestic price was not presented.

The federal Oil Policy Committee was then formed to deal with policy issues within the quota framework. (Formerly, the secretary of the interior had handled the oil import program. Under this arrangement, a number of dubious decisions had been made suggesting allocation of import rights on a highly political and partisan basis.[25]) Management of quotas by an interagency committee provided an image of stability and continuity. But the decisions of the committee had a different effect. In the first place, the quotas were expanded at an increasingly rapid rate. And second, special exemptions were given to petrochemical plants and independent fuel terminal operators after heavy political pressure from the petrochemical industry and New England congressmen. On top of this, crude oil prices were held down by informal pressures up until August 1971 and by compulsory price controls thereafter. In form the industry still had a quota program and market-demand prorationing, all the trappings of the earlier cartel. In practice it had control of neither price nor domestic production, for the policy in force required that imports be expanded sufficiently to keep domestic prices down.

Under these circumstances the domestic refining and producing industry could not be certain whether the future held unlimited imports at reduced prices or genuine import restrictions and higher domestic prices. This uncertainty led to the only prudent conduct that could be expected: complaints about the lack of clearly defined energy policy and avoidance of investments in U.S. crude production or refining until the policy became evident. The administration never really made an explicit policy decision on imports. The movement of domestic crude production to capacity and the rise of world oil prices to the domestic level made the quotas ineffective, and in the spring of 1973 they were scrapped.

When the world price passed the U.S. price, a policy decision had to be made. Do we have a free-market policy in oil or a shortage policy, with prices set below the market-clearing level? The shortage policy was chosen. New crude oil prices have been freed, but old crude oil prices remain controlled. With price controls on refining and marketing margins, petroleum product prices are below the market-clearing level.

Oil policy has turned 180 degrees since 1969. In that year consumers paid about $6 billion *more* for oil than they would have paid in a free market. Today, domestic crude producers receive roughly $11 billion *less* per year than they would receive in a free market.[26] If we are concerned not with what each special interest

---

[25] This is all covered in various issues of the *Oil and Gas Journal* in the mid- and late sixties. A useful summary is K. Dam's "Implementation of Quotas: The Case of Oil," *The Journal of Law and Economics*, vol. 14, no. 1 (April 1971).

[26] This is calculated by multiplying the difference between the delivered foreign crude price (roughly $9.50 per barrel) and the domestic crude price (roughly $6.50 per barrel) by the annual domestic production (currently running at roughly 3.6 billion barrels per year, including natural gas liquids).

group lost or gained but what was lost or gained by the nation as a whole then these are not the figures to concentrate on. Import quotas cost consumers $6 billion per year, but they benefitted producers significantly less, resulting in a national waste of $1 billion per year or more. Today's policy of low domestic crude prices is also wasting the nation's resources, as consumer benefits certainly fall short of producer losses, probably by more than a billion dollars per year. Perhaps the most consistent element in U.S. oil policy is economic inefficiency.

4

NATURAL GAS:
FROM FREE MARKET
TO SHORTAGE POLICY

Natural gas is largely a phenomenon of the last two decades. Prior to World War II there was no economical way of transporting gas more than moderate distances. Markets were confined to the immediate producing area. With the development of economical long-distance pipelines, the large natural gas reserves discovered in the search for oil became available nationwide as fast as pipelines and distribution systems could be constructed. In 1946, 4.9 trillion cubic feet (tcf) were produced in the United States. By 1970 this had risen more than fourfold to 22 tcf.

Natural gas has two basic markets: the residential and commercial market, where it is used for heating homes and offices, cooking, and hot water heating; and the industrial and electric utility market, where it is a boiler fuel used to produce direct heat or steam for industrial processes and electricity generation. In the residential and commercial market, which accounted for 33 percent of total gas consumption in 1968, gas competes mainly with home heating oil. In the industrial and electric utility market, 64 percent of consumption in 1968, it competes with coal and heavy fuel oil (as well as hydro and nuclear energy sources in the electric utility sector). The remaining 3 percent of natural gas production is used in the transportation sector.

Natural gas is produced in the same states by essentially the same companies that produce crude oil. Like crude oil, today natural gas in the field is sold in a competitive market. Entry into the industry is easy, concentration is low, and statistical studies of prices confirm the lack of influence over price by individual firms.[1]

---

[1] See P. MacAvoy, *Price Formation in Natural Gas Fields* (New Haven: Yale University Press, 1962); Clark Hawkins, *The Field Price Regulation of Natural Gas* (Tallahassee: Florida State University Press, 1969); E. Kitch, "Regulation and

Natural gas differs from crude oil dramatically in the degree of government price regulation. Oil prices (before the August 1971 price controls) were not regulated at the wellhead, at the refinery, or at the retail outlet. Common carrier pipeline oil transportation is regulated by the Interstate Commerce Commission, but most oil is moved by tanker, barge, or company-owned trucks. Prices for natural gas sold in interstate commerce are regulated at the wellhead by the Federal Power Commission. Interstate gas pipelines are also regulated by the FPC, and local gas distribution companies are regulated by state public utility commissions. Thus, from the wellhead to the basement furnace, prices of natural gas sold in interstate commerce are under government control.

The rationale for gas pipeline and distribution regulation is that there are positive returns to scale in both activities which would lead to a private monopoly in the absence of regulation. This is presumed to be worse from a public point of view than a regulated, government-imposed monopoly. Whatever the merits of this argument, the basis for regulating wellhead prices, as distinct from pipelines and distribution prices, has always been controversial and puzzling to say the least. As noted above, the crude oil and natural gas producing industries are very similar from the point of view of the firms involved and the degree of concentration of production.

Evolution of the Present Regulatory System

In 1938 Congress passed the Natural Gas Act for the purpose of placing pipelines selling natural gas in interstate commerce under the regulatory authority of the Federal Power Commission. The act was specifically made inapplicable "to the production or gathering of natural gas." Sales of gas at the wellhead by independent producers thus continued unregulated by the FPC until the 1954 Supreme Court decision in *Phillips Petroleum Co.* v. *Wisconsin.* In this decision, the Court concluded that Phillips, although engaged solely in production and gathering operations, was a "natural gas company" within the meaning of the Natural Gas Act and that its sales for resale in inter-

the Field Market for Natural Gas," *Journal of Law and Economics*, vol. 11 (October 1968); Norman Ture, "Testimony submitted on Behalf of the Gas Supply Committee to the Subcommittee on Antitrust and Monopoly," Committee on the Judiciary, U.S. Senate, 27 June 1973, mimeographed; Clark Hawkins, "Structure of the Natural Gas Producing Industry," in Keith Brown, ed., *Regulation of the Natural Gas Producing Industry* (Baltimore: The Johns Hopkins University Press, 1972); L. Cookenboo, "Competition in the Field Market for Natural Gas," *The Rice Institute Pamphlet*, vol. 44, no. 4 (January 1958); and E. Neuner, *The Natural Gas Industry* (Norman: University of Oklahoma Press, 1960).

state commerce were subject to FPC regulation. Natural gas produced and consumed within a state was not made subject to regulation.

Thereafter, attempts by the FPC to regulate the over 4,000 independent producers on a company-by-company basis resulted in a backlog so great that in 1960 the FPC was described by a former Harvard Law School dean as "the outstanding example in the Federal government of the breakdown of the Administrative process."[2] Recognizing the virtual impossibility of regulating each company individually, the commission initiated the area rate theory of regulation in 1960. Instead of determining the rates that each producer would be permitted to charge for selling its natural gas, the FPC stated that all gas sold in a particular producing area would be valued on a "commodity" basis.

In 1961 the FPC commenced the *Permian Basin Area Rate Proceeding*, which it completed in 1965. In 1968 the Supreme Court affirmed the commission's opinion and orders in this case as being within the FPC's administrative discretion.[3]

The *Permian* methodology used by the FPC to arrive at the rates which it would allow producers to receive was an adaptation of the utility rate-base, cost-of-service approach. This approach had been developed over the past half century for rate regulation of public utility monopolies, such as the gas pipelines and electric power companies. In developing the costs to be applied in determining the rate base and cost of service, the FPC attempted to use the average, composite costs of the entire producing industry. Since this data was not available, the FPC elicited the information from industry through the use of massive questionnaires. After compiling the responses, the commission then attempted the logically impossible task of allocating costs between the joint production of oil and gas. Confronted with a wide range of choices in making its cost calculations, the FPC made determinations to the nearest mill, invariably selecting figures which were at the lower end of the spectrum. The commission then applied a 12 percent rate of return and established "just and reasonable" ceiling rates for all gas produced from the Permian Basin area.

One economist specializing in gas regulation matters has written that

> it is quite beyond the FPC or anyone else to determine what is the cost of natural gas for an integrated producer. Let alone

---

[2] As quoted in U.S. Department of the Interior, "Natural Gas," an in-house background report cited in *Natural Gas Deregulation* (Washington, D. C.: American Enterprise Institute, 1973), p. 11.

[3] Permian Area Rate Cases, 390 U.S. 747 (1968).

for a segment of the industry [*sic*]. The way those present-
ing data and calculations of average cost of an MCF of gas
in area hearings switch back and forth among sources, the
way they make joint cost allocations, and the way they
apply "factors" represent pseudo-science to a degree it would
be difficult to equal by example. At the final determination
the examiner's fumbling among the numbers and making
a cafeteria style selection from those presented, plus the
Commission adding a few delicate adjustments of its own
makes the whole thing nothing short of ludicrous.[4]

The *Permian* decision also introduced a concept which became
known as "vintaging." Gas dedicated to interstate commerce by
contract prior to a certain date was known as "old," or "flowing,"
gas, while gas dedicated by contract at a later date was known as
"new" gas. A higher ceiling was permitted for the new gas on the
theory that this would provide incentive for future exploration.
Vintaging has been criticized on the ground that the consumer has
no interest in the date the gas was dedicated to interstate commerce:
an old cubic foot burns as well as a new one. Additionally, it has
operated to provide existing pipeline companies which have contracts
to purchase large volumes of "old" gas with an advantage over newer
pipeline companies which have to contract for the more expensive
"new" gas. Similarly, customers of pipeline companies with a higher
percentage of "new" gas volumes pay more for their purchases than
customers of pipelines with contracts providing more "old" gas
supplies.

In establishing "just and reasonable" rates, the FPC attempted
to determine average costs within the industry, thus making it difficult
for high-cost producers (generally those with a less fortuitous finding
rate) to compete. However, while forcing down contracts that were
priced above the "average cost," the commission did not counter-
balance this by permitting lower-priced contracts to rise to the "just
and reasonable" rate. Although it established minimum rates that
were generally below almost every contract in the area, the FPC
generally limited producers to their contract rates when these were
lower than the area rate.

In 1968 the FPC, using the same methodology, established area
rates for southern Louisiana. This time, however, the commission
was even more restrictive than in the *Permian* proceeding. Area rates

---

[4] Clark Hawkins, "Structure of the Natural Gas Producing Industry," in *Regulation of the Natural Gas Producing Industry*, ed. K. Brown (Baltimore: The Johns
Hopkins University Press, 1972), p. 165.

were established below what the commission had previously set as guidelines for producers, and the industry was ordered to refund hundreds of millions of dollars for collecting "excessive" rates in prior years.

Completions of new gas wells declined steadily after 1962, the year after the commencement of the *Permian Basin* proceedings. In each of the four years subsequent to the 1968 *Southern Louisiana* decision, the domestic consumption of natural gas exceeded the American Gas Association's estimates of new additions to reserves in the lower forty-eight states.

Since 1969 the FPC has taken some steps to mitigate the developing shortages. In 1971 the second area rate decision in *Southern Louisiana* raised the area rates by approximately 30 percent. Other area rate proceedings established rates consistent with that decision. Natural gas discoveries increased by 32 percent in 1972 and by 40 percent for the first nine months of 1973.[5] This, however, appears to be largely a response to rising unregulated intrastate shipment (except that coming from federal offshore leases).

The Natural Gas Shortage

Between 1946 and 1960 natural gas production rose from 4.9 to 13 tcf per year. At the same time the American Gas Association's estimate of proved reserves rose from 159.7 to 262.3 tcf. The reserve-production ratio thus fell from 32.5 to 20.1. These movements can be explained in elementary economic terms. Between 1946 and 1960 the real price of natural gas at the wellhead rose appreciably, and expectations during the period were for rising prices. These rising prices were due to the expanding gas markets spurred by the development of long-distance pipeline technology, and they spurred a continuing search for gas and additions to the stock of proved reserves.

The reserve-production ratio desired by producers depends upon the relationship between expected future prices and current prices. Producers will hold more reserves (inventories) if future prices are expected to be high relative to current prices. The fall in the actual reserve-production ratio indicates that it was above that desired by producers throughout the period, and that producers did not expand reserves as rapidly as production in order to lower the ratio to its target level.

---

[5] Statement of Stephen Wakefield, assistant secretary of the interior, before the Special Subcommittee on Integrated Oil Operations, Committee on Interior and Insular Affairs, United States Senate, 28 November 1973.

Figure 1

RATIO OF NATURAL GAS RESERVES TO PRODUCTION IN THE
UNITED STATES FROM 1950 TO 1971

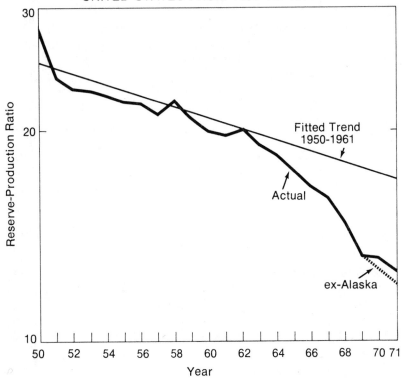

Source: American Gas Association, "Reserves of Crude Oil, Natural Gas Liquids, and Natural Gas in the United States and Canada and United States Productive Capacity as of December 31, 1971," vol. 26 (Arlington, Va., May 1972).

In 1961 the *Permian* hearings began. In the ensuing years it became evident that expectations of higher wellhead prices would have to be revised. The course of prices after 1961 completely reinforced that view, and real wellhead prices for "new" gas in 1969 were below the 1961 level. Whatever the target reserve-production ratio that was being approached prior to 1961, the target clearly must have been lowered with the advent of regulation. Prices were now expected to either rise at a lower rate or actually fall. With the target reserve-production ratio lowered, the rate of decline in the actual ratio accelerated. From 1950 to 1962 the ratio fell by 2.3 percent per year, and from 1963 to 1971 it fell at 4.3 percent per year, almost twice the earlier rate. These trends are shown in Figure 1.

Thus, for given reserves the price ceiling imposed by the FPC accelerated domestic production. Owners of reserves no longer expected future prices to yield an adequate return for holding reserves. The ceilings also reduced the incentive to explore for and develop new reserves. Despite the fact that future demand would obviously be much greater than current demand, reserve additions were below production every year the four years succeeding the 1968 *Southern Louisiana* decision. These trends in production and reserve additions could not continue indefinitely without creating a shortage in current supply. Dating the beginning of the shortage to consumers is not easy, but it probably occurred somewhere between 1968 and 1970. More important is the fact that the divergence between actual and free-market conditions occurred somewhere around 1963 when the *Permian* decisions were becoming clear, prices were beginning to level off, and the reserve-production ratio decline began to accelerate.

While this discussion gives us a feeling for when problems in the natural gas market began and what the causes of those problems were, it does not tell us how large the shortage is or what the market would have looked like in the absence of ceiling prices. The only serious attempts to simulate the natural gas market in the absence of regulation are those of Paul W. MacAvoy. In one paper he sets up an econometric model of the market and simulates the post-*Permian* period using market parameters estimated in the pre-*Permian* period.[6] In a more recent paper he develops a more complex model and simulates the late 1970s assuming, alternatively, continued regulation and a freeing of new contract prices as would occur under the President's deregulation bill.[7]

Although MacAvoy's 1971 model does not correspond exactly to the economic logic set out above, his qualitative results with regard to prices, reserve additions, and the reserve-production ratio confirm the interpretation in eastern and midwestern natural gas markets. MacAvoy concludes that under free-market conditions new-contract prices would have been more than double actual regulated prices from 1964 to 1967, new reserves added would have been 40 percent larger than reserves added at the ceiling prices, and the reserve-production ratio would have been substantially higher over the period.

The comparative levels of production under regulation and free markets is ambiguous in economic theory. MacAvoy's model suggests that production would have been slightly higher under free

---

[6] Paul W. MacAvoy, "The Regulation Induced Shortage of Natural Gas," *The Journal of Law and Economics*, vol. 14, no. 1 (April 1971), pp. 167-199.

[7] MacAvoy and Pindyck, "Alternative Regulatory Policies," pp. 454-498.

markets than under regulation, the results varying from year to year. Of course, in the long run, production under free markets would become continuously greater than under regulation because reserve levels would continuously diverge while the reserve-production ratios would tend to stabilize. MacAvoy's simulation extends only to 1967 and therefore does not reveal this trend.

It is not possible to adequately treat MacAvoy's complex econometric model in a monograph such as this. However, in the case of the shortage of reserve additions brought about by regulation, a ballpark figure can be arrived at by a much cruder analysis. Suppose we assume that the 2.3 percent annual decline in the reserve-production ratio of the 1950 to 1962 period had continued to 1967, and that annual production had been the same. Then by 1967 U.S. natural gas reserves would have been 319 trillion cubic feet instead of the actual 293 tcf. Reserve additions over the period would have been close to 130 tcf as compared with an actual 102 tcf—28 percent greater. If we extend this analysis to 1971, the reserve additions would have been 58 percent greater under the free market. These figures bracket Mac-Avoy's 40 percent shortage estimated for eastern and midwestern markets. Thus, by either sophisticated or very crude methods it can be concluded that new reserves added fell far short of what could be expected in a free market.

MacAvoy's more recent model simulates the gas market for the remainder of the 1970s. He considers three scenarios: (1) deregulation of new-contract prices with a national ceiling that would keep average wholesale prices from rising more than 50 percent over a five-year period, (2) strict "cost of service" regulation based on historical average costs, and (3) continuation of the current policy of allowing increases of two to four cents per thousand cubic feet each year. Under either "strict cost" regulation, or the status quo, the gas shortage continues through the 1970s. In the strict cost case the shortage grows from 4 tcf in 1972 to 8.9 tcf in 1980. In the status quo case the shortage grows from 4 to 5.3 tcf. In the deregulation case the shortage disappears in 1977.[8]

From the standpoint of economic efficiency these shortages—past, present, and future—represent social waste. Opportunities are eliminated for exchange between producers willing to develop and sell gas at prices higher than ceilings and consumers whose valuation of the gas exceeds the price ceilings. This production and consumption never takes place. Instead, these consumers must use less fuel or

---

[8] Ibid.

pay at least twice the free-market wellhead price for gasified coal or for liquified natural gas imports, or use more expensive alternative fuels.

Distributive Effects of Regulation

While the costs of regulation clearly exceed the benefits from an overall societal point of view, few policies are decided on this basis. It is common to advocate inefficient policies when they have "desirable" consequences for the distribution of income. Whatever the merits of these judgments about the relative moral worth of different individuals and groups, it is important to examine the distributional consequences of any policy. Many people believe they are important and, above all, the political process responds to such considerations.

The distributive consequences of FPC price regulation are dominated by one consideration: some people who would be paying more for natural gas in a free market are paying lower prices and getting gas. Others who would be willing to pay the ceiling price, or the free-market price, or even more, are not getting gas. They must either do without fuel or purchase more expensive or less desirable alternatives. The favored group consists of those who are rationed gas by interstate pipelines and those who buy gas in the intrastate market exempt from FPC regulation. Intrastate consumers are not now as favored as interstate consumers because intrastate prices have risen above the interstate level. But interstate consumers of gas are a dwindling group, since the low interstate prices attract little new gas from producers to replace dwindling supplies.

Only one-third of the natural gas sold is consumed by residential and commercial users. Nevertheless, in political terms this must be the group that the FPC is intending to benefit with low prices. Yet studies by MacAvoy and Stephen Breyer have indicated that it is not residential and commercial users but rather industrial users that have benefitted from low ceiling prices.[9] With the development of shortages, pipelines and distribution companies apparently devoted supplies to industrial users rather than connecting new residential and commercial users. The explanation for this diversion of supplies is that the FPC and many states do not regulate industrial sales of gas. Since industrial users are less "protected" by the regulatory authorities than homeowners, they get the gas and the new homeowner does

---

[9] P. MacAvoy and Stephen Breyer, "The Natural Gas Shortage and the Regulation of Natural Gas Producers," *Harvard Law Review*, April 1973.

without. This shifting of artificially cheap natural gas supplies to the industrial sector has apparently been very profitable for natural gas pipelines. The author has computed that a stockholder who bought the Standard and Poor's sixty utilities at the end of 1965 would have realized an 18.1 percent increase in the value of his holdings by the end of 1972, assuming he had reinvested his dividends. If he had instead invested in the Standard and Poor's natural gas pipeline stocks, he would have realized a 55.5 percent gain over the same period.[10]

A few statistics illustrate what has been happening. From 1950 to 1957, a period of rapid industrial expansion, gas consumption in the residential market grew at 10.9 percent compared with 9.4 percent in the industrial sector. From 1957 to 1962 both growth rates declined, but residential consumption growth widened its margin over industrial consumption, 7.5 percent to 4.8 percent. From 1962 to 1968, when price regulation began to take effect, the growth rate of residential consumption fell to 5.5 percent, but the rate of industrial consumption accelerated to 6.6 percent.

Another way of addressing the question is to compare how gas did in each of its markets relative to overall energy consumption in those markets. Between 1962 and 1968 total gas consumption grew faster than overall energy consumption. (As we have seen, this was because reserves were being depleted faster, not because they were becoming more abundant.)

Table 5 shows the market share of natural gas in five energy sectors in 1962 (at the start of the *Permian* hearings) and in 1968. In every energy market except the residential, gas increased its share. In the residential sector gas lost ground to electricity, a far more expensive source of heat. (This may be, at least in part, the result of a shift in the marketing tactics of electric utilities.) With the exception of the New England and Middle Atlantic states, 80 to 90 percent of the homes in all regions of the country were heating with gas in 1968. My estimates of the comparative economics of oil and gas heating in these areas suggest that gas was more economical in the Middle Atlantic states and roughly competitive in New England. In New York City in 1970 the cost of generating a btu for homes using oil appeared to be about one-third greater than the cost of using gas when incremental capital costs of oil heating are taken into account. Rougher estimates for seven other cities in the Middle Atlantic region suggest a 25 to 30 percent advantage for gas.[11] While gas heating

---

[10] Dividends were assumed to be reinvested at the succeeding year's closing price.
[11] A far more detailed research project would be required to ascertain with confidence the comparative costs of alternative heating systems to the homeowner.

Table 5

MARKET SHARE OF NATURAL GAS AS A PERCENTAGE
OF TOTAL ENERGY CONSUMPTION IN
EACH ENERGY MARKET

Market	1962	1968
Residential	50.7%	50.1%
Commercial	21.5	26.8
Industrial	40.4	43.3
Transportation	.35	.4
Electric utilities	25.9	26.1

Source: Stanford Research Institute, "Pattern of Energy Consumption in the United States," mimeographed, November 1971, various tables.

raised its share of households in the Middle Atlantic market from 12 percent in 1950 to 35 percent in 1960, its share had increased to only 47 percent by 1968.[12]

The shortages of natural gas to residential users mean that there is a greater demand for alternative fuels, namely, home heating oil and electricity, to heat homes. Since the supply of these alternatives is not perfectly elastic, this added demand must have increased prices beyond what they would have been if gas prices were unregulated. (The introduction of price controls in August 1971 has resulted in shortages in place of higher prices.) Thus, homeowners heating with oil or electricity must be worse off as compared to a free natural gas market. Table 5 shows that this group was approximately equal in size (when weighted by consumption) to the favored gas-consuming group in 1968, but growing faster. Thus we would expect more current statistics to show that more households (weighted by consumption) were made worse off by FPC price controls than were made better off.

One group clearly benefitted by FPC regulation of *interstate* prices is *intrastate* gas users. Because they are not "protected" by FPC controls, consumers in Texas, Louisiana, Oklahoma, and other large producing states can outbid New York and Chicago purchasers and obtain all the gas they want. And because the potential demand of interstate buyers is eliminated at prices above the ceilings, the effective national demand for natural gas is lower than it would be otherwise.

---

[12] In New England the market share of natural gas rose to 44 percent in 1968. Consideration of the poorer economics of gas versus oil heating in New England suggests a noneconomic allocation of supplies between New England and the Middle Atlantic.

The free-market intrastate price, therefore, is lower than it would be in a totally free national market. Thus intrastate gas users not only get all the gas they want, but get it at a price that is lower because of FPC attempts to protect *all other* gas consumers. This is one of those ironies so common to ill-conceived economic policies. But the ultimate irony is the bill before Congress to "solve the gas shortage" by extending FPC regulation to the intrastate market.[13] Having unintentionally bestowed benefits on some gas consumers, some senators and congressmen apparently feel they must correct that oversight and impose gas shortages on everyone—on grounds of fairness, of course.

The lower prices and lack of shortages in large gas producing states benefit not only gas users in those states, but also complementary factors of production. Armco Steel's decision to locate a plant in Texas because of an assured gas supply benefits Texas workers. Intrastate pipelines, such as Lone Star, have experienced dramatic growth that would not have occurred in a free national market. Conversely, complementary factors of production outside the major producing states have been injured—the 30,000 workers laid off for ten days in Cleveland in January 1970, to cite one early example.[14] The number of plants that were not built in gas-shortage areas will never be known.

The environmental consequences of regulation-induced gas shortages have not gone unnoticed. Natural gas is a far cleaner fuel than the cleanest heavy oil or coal, particularly with regard to sulfur content. Not only is the quality of air reduced overall by gas shortages, but the regional distribution of dirty air is distorted. Partly because New York and Chicago cannot compete against Dallas and Houston for gas supplies, 1975 clean air standards cannot be met. According to the Environmental Protection Agency, a four-fold increase in natural gas supplies to New York City would be required to meet the standards for atmospheric particulates. There is no possibility of this occurring under the present regulatory approach.

Arguments Against Deregulation

Two arguments have been made against deregulation. One is that the natural gas producing industry is monopolistic and cannot be

---

13 See S. 2506, the Consumer Energy Act of 1974, 93d Congress, 1st and 2d sessions. The use of the word "consumer" in the title of this bill is clearly deceptive advertising if it is supposed to indicate the benefitted party.

14 MacAvoy and Pindyck, "Alternative Regulatory Policies," p. 455.

permitted to exploit consumers by charging monopoly prices. This position has been advanced by some staff members of the Federal Power Commission.[15] The position and its supporting arguments have been dismissed by economists specializing in energy markets, such as Professors Adelman, Hawkins, MacAvoy, and Russell,[16] and, of course, contradicted by the studies cited earlier.[17] By every accepted measure—concentration, entry, market tactics, prices, profits—the industry is competitive, and, in some respects, it is among the more competitive of American industries. To argue monopoly in this case is to argue monopoly for most of the U.S. economy, an argument that falls of its own weight. Only in the realm of politics and journalism could the monopoly thesis survive.

The other argument against deregulation assumes the market is competitive but that natural gas supply is not sensitive to price. Higher prices would, therefore, mean greater earnings for producers but little additional supply for consumers. According to this line of reasoning, ceiling prices below the market-clearing level would result in shortages, but they would be small and manageable. While inefficiencies in the allocation of resources would result, they would be more than offset by the "positive" distributive effects on income. Note that advocacy of this shortage policy is based on the value judgment that consumers who are allocated gas are sufficiently more worthy than consumers who are not allocated gas (and, of course, gas producers) so that some small cost in economic efficiency is worth paying.

This argument, made by Professor Alfred Kahn during the *Permian* hearings,[18] is premised on one empirically testable proposition: the response of natural gas supply to price is small. Unfortunately, at the time the argument was made, little research had been done on the question. In the past several years a number of studies have been carried out. All show that the response of supply to price has been and is likely to be substantial. Thus, low ceiling prices

[15] Testimony of J. Wilson and D. Schwartz before the Subcommittee on Antitrust and Monopoly, Committee on the Judiciary, U.S. Senate, 27 June 1973.

[16] For the list of academic supporters of the competitive view, see Committee on Interior and Insular Affairs, United States Senate, *Natural Gas Policy Issues and Options: A Staff Analysis* (Washington, D.C.: Government Printing Office, 1973), p. 84.

[17] Footnote 1 of this chapter.

[18] Alfred Kahn, *In the Matter of Area Rate Proceeding*, Docket No. AR 61-1, Federal Power Commission, and "Economic Issues in Regulating the Field Price of Natural Gas," *American Economic Review*, May 1960. Professor Kahn seems to have revised his opinions in view of the shortages.

imply large shortages and injure many consumers as well as producers. Indeed, as suggested above, the number of consumers injured (weighted by consumption) may well exceed the number benefited.

Natural Gas Supply Response to Price

Because many would not be prepared to deregulate gas prices unless they had reasonable assurance of a substantial supply response, we now turn to a more extensive discussion of what the various supply models show. Five estimates were made of the response of gas supply to price. These estimates are based on five independent studies or models (not including the latest MacAvoy model, which has already been discussed): (1) the National Petroleum Council (NPC) model, constructed by a team of technicians from several major oil companies for use by the Department of the Interior, (2) the Khazzoom model, developed under contract for the Federal Power Commission by Professor J. Daniel Khazzoom,[19] (3) the Erickson-Spann model, published by two university professors in *The Bell Journal of Economics and Management Science*,[20] (4) the early MacAvoy model, published in the *Journal of Law and Economics*,[21] and (5) the Garrett study, a paper on the quantity of recoverable gas economical at various wellhead prices, presented to the Potential Gas Committee by Ralph Garrett of Exxon Corporation.[22]

Projections were made directly from the first two models, given alternative assumptions about price. At the request of the author, the NPC made the projection from its model and the FPC staff made the projection from the Khazzoom model. Each of the other three studies leads to an estimate of the price elasticity of gas supply. These elasticities were utilized separately in a simple supply projection model constructed by the author. The projections made from these latter elasticities, therefore, depend not only on the elasticities themselves but also on the method of projection.

For each of these models two cases are considered:

Base Case: Wellhead price of natural gas constant at twenty-four cents per thousand cubic feet (mcf).

---

[19] J. D. Khazzoom, "The FPC Staff's Econometric Model of Natural Gas Supply in the United States," *The Bell Journal of Economics and Management Science*, vol. 2, no. 1 (Spring 1971).
[20] E. Erickson and R. Spann, "Supply Price in a Regulated Industry: The Case of Natural Gas," in ibid.
[21] MacAvoy, "Regulation Induced Shortage of Natural Gas."
[22] R. Garrett, "Effect of Prices on Future Natural Gas Supplies."

Deregulation Case: Wellhead price of natural gas rises to sixty-five cents per mcf (assumed free-market level) immediately and at 2.5 percent per year thereafter.

The assumption of a gas price of sixty-five cents per mcf after deregulation is consistent with recent uncontrolled intrastate prices, with MacAvoy's recent model, and with the Garrett study. Note that this is well below the costs of imported liquified natural gas and synthetic gas from coal or oil, which generally run $1.00 to $1.50 per mcf or more (wellhead equivalent).

While the assumption of a sixty-five cent wellhead price is useful for comparing the response of supply in different models, it has to be recognized that the response of gas supply will partially determine the price. In a free market price and quantity are determined simultaneously. This means that a model that forecasts a strong supply response to price is also forecasting that a smaller increase in price is required to clear the market. Furthermore, consumption of competing fuels, such as low-sulfur residual oil, home heating oil, and coal, will be depressed by the added gas supplies, and the prices of these fuels will be reduced.

Before laying out the supply schedules generated by these models, a brief description of how each model works is in order. The NPC model translates drilling footage into new reserves by means of a careful analysis of historical relationships between footage drilled and reserves discovered for fourteen different regions of the U.S. Each region has a separate engineering model with different parameters based on different historical experience and potential. For each region the model generates reserves, production, and capital and operating expenditures for any given drilling rate. For the industry to be in equilibrium, the flow of income from all production, old and new, must be such that, when compared to the total book value of capital, it yields a rate of return acceptable to the industry. The latter can be varied in the model. For the NPC forecast it was set at 15 percent return after taxes. Price is the variable that is adjusted so as to make the rate of return come out to 15 percent for a given drilling rate. Thus, there is a connection established between drilling rate (and hence production) and price. But it is drilling that "causes" price in the NPC model—not the other way around. Apparently one of the reasons for building the model "backwards" was to avoid the antitrust problem: the companies could not collectively agree on assumed prices.

To deal with the two cases the model had to be run backwards. Essentially what was done to find the pattern of drilling rate over time that yielded price patterns resembling the two cases. The model involves a choice of optimistic or pessimistic success rates in drilling, and the author averaged these two alternatives.

The Khazzoom, Erickson and Spann, and MacAvoy models are all econometric models. An equation, or set of equations, is postulated that represents the behavior of the industry as it responds to changes in price and other variables. Then the parameters of these equations are estimated by "fitting" the equations to the numerical data from some historical period: Khazzoom uses the period 1961-68, Erickson and Spann, 1946-59, and MacAvoy, 1954-60. All arrive at the conclusion that gas supply responds significantly to price. Erickson and Spann's elasticity of supply estimate is .69, meaning that a 10 percent increase in price yields a 6.9 percent increase in new reserves found. MacAvoy's estimate is .45. Neither the Khazzoom model nor the industry model yields a constant elasticity of supply.

To the elasticities of Erickson-Spann and MacAvoy can be added another estimate derived from the work of Garrett of Exxon Corporation. He estimated the quantities of potentially discoverable reserves that would be economical at various prices. The elasticity of his curve between current prices and seventy cents per mcf is roughly .6. If it is assumed that the industry tends to find in any year a constant fraction of the total reserves worth producing at contemporary prices, then a given percentage increase in price has the same proportional effect on reserve additions each year as it has on ultimately recoverable reserves. On this assumption Garrett's elasticity can be used in the same way as the others. It should be stressed, however, that this assumption is made by the author and is not implicit in the Garrett study.

To develop projections from these three estimates of elasticity of supply, it was assumed that the reserves added in 1969, 1970, and 1971 were in response to the 1966-70 FPC authorized price of eighteen cents per mcf. Any given percentage change in price was then translated into reserve additions by applying the particular elasticity to the 1969-71 reserve-addition data. For example, a 100 percent increase in price in 1973 would result in a 60 percent greater quantity of reserves added if the elasticity were .6. The reserve-production ratio was assumed to be ten to one in 1975 and thereafter. This type of projection has been labelled a constant elasticity of supply (CES) projection.

Table 6 gives the figures for the five projections of natural gas supply for the two cases. Only one projection is shown in the base

Table 6

NATURAL GAS PRODUCTION
(trillions of cubic feet)

Study	1970	1975	1980	1985
Base Case				
NPC	22.0	18.8	13.5	8.6
CES	22.0	19.9	16.4	14.4
Khazzoom	22.0	18.0	17.0	16.6
Deregulation Case				
NPC	22.0	24.1	26.9	30.5
CES:				
e = .5 (MacAvoy)	22.0	24.0	24.4	25.7
e = .6 (Garrett)	22.0	24.7	26.1	28.2
e = .7 (Erickson)	22.0	25.4	27.8	30.7
Khazzoom	22.0	20.5	27.3	31.5

case for the three CES projections because they are very similar in that case.

In the base case every model shows production falling. Khazzoom is the most optimistic with a drop from 22 tcf in 1970 to 16.6 tcf in 1985. CES shows a drop to 14.4 tcf by 1985, and NPC is most pessimistic with a predicted drop to 8.6 tcf.

In the deregulation case production increases in each model. The smallest gains came from MacAvoy's early model, just 3.7 tcf per year more in 1985 than in 1970. The largest gains came from the Khazzoom model, an increase of 9.5 tcf in 1985 over 1970.

But the question relevant to this discussion is: How much more natural gas is supplied in the deregulation case than in the base case? Taking each model separately, the smallest difference in 1985 between the two options is 11.3 tcf (early MacAvoy) and the largest is 21.9 tcf (NPC). These are enormous magnitudes. Converting these figures to oil equivalents, the smallest difference is 5.5 million barrels per day and the largest is 10.7 million barrels per day. For perspective, consider that in 1972 total U.S. oil imports were 4.7 million barrels per day and total U.S. crude oil production was 9.5 million barrels per day. While any modeling of this sort must be taken with some skepticism, the fact that five independent studies (some using totally different analytical frameworks) conclude that supplies will be much larger under deregulation is hard to ignore.

5

SUMMARY
AND CONCLUSIONS

The shortage of energy now facing the nation is not a problem for public policy—it is a public policy. Shortages can be eliminated very simply: remove price controls on energy. The task for policy makers is to make energy less scarce and less costly. This means removing artificial scarcities created by price controls and reversing the policy of hoarding the nation's resources by government.

Are energy resources growing more scarce? There is no evidence that energy will be as scarce in the long run as current market conditions seem to suggest. Any forecast of future energy consumption and costs is extremely speculative. What knowledge we do have of future supplies suggests that they may cost more than we are accustomed to but not so much more as to result in dramatic changes in styles of living.

Why is there an energy crisis? One thesis is a spontaneous acceleration in demand. While the fact is that consumption growth accelerated in the late 1960s the data suggest that this acceleration was not so much a result of economic growth or exogenous forces as of consumption induced by rapidly falling prices. The acceleration in price decline was in large part the consequence of shifts in public policy over the past decade rather than a growing abundance of energy resources.

These public policies tended to stimulate current consumption while discouraging the discovery of energy reserves that would provide for future demand. The inevitable consequence of these policies was an artificial scarcity of energy that became obvious to the consumer only in 1973.

One of the major reasons for continuing error in energy policy making is a false perception of the problem. The view that public policy must address itself to gaps between supply and demand is resulting in support for policies that have little social value and great social cost. Much of energy research and development activity, such as the aggressive coal gasification programs, falls into this category. The large-scale importation of liquified natural gas from overseas is an example of another activity artificially stimulated by government but indefensible on public interest grounds.

The history of U.S. oil policy is one of surplus policies in the 1950s and '60s evolving into a shortage policy in the 1970s. This shift appears to be due mainly to movements in political sentiment and influence and not to changes in energy resource conditions. Neither shortage nor surplus policies are in the public interest, and particularly not in the consumer's interest.

The principal devices by which surplus policies were effected were market-demand prorationing and the import quota system. These permitted higher crude oil prices to prevail in the domestic market than abroad by restricting both domestic production and imports. The surplus policy hurt consumers. It also injured more efficient producers by raising the cost of production from efficient wells. The principal beneficiaries appear to have been small inefficient stripper-well producers.

In 1970 this surplus policy began to change. Import quotas were expanded rapidly. Domestic crude prices were held down, at first by informal pressures and then, in 1971, by strict price controls. By April 1972 all U.S. productive capacity was in use, and all incremental demands had to be met by imports. In early 1973 world prices reached the domestic level as the cartel of producing nations achieved remarkable successes in raising prices. At this point the quota program no longer served a useful purpose, and it was scrapped.

Later in 1973 the world price passed the domestic price and a crucial decision had to be made: adopt a free-market or a shortage policy. The U.S. government chose shortages. Facing the same choice, many European governments chose essentially free markets, avoiding shortages.

To deal with the world cartel and artificially high world oil prices, the United States should adopt policies that make U.S. imports highly sensitive to the cartel price, thereby creating incentives for lower prices. The domestic price controls have the opposite effect in that they subsidize high import prices with artificially cheap domestic oil.

One of the major causes of the artificial scarcity of energy in the United States is the extraordinarily low regulated price of natural gas.

Natural gas is the largest single domestic source of energy and accounted for a large part of the growth in energy consumption since 1950. But much of the gas produced in recent decades was discovered before 1950 in the search for oil. Since the imposition of strict Federal Power Commission price regulation in 1960, discoveries have fallen off substantially.

The natural gas shortage policy is one of the least defensible economic policies in American history. Attempts to justify the shortage on grounds of keeping consumer prices low fail because most consumers have to pay higher prices for alternative fuels, and because the benefitted group will steadily dwindle in numbers. The principal beneficiaries appear to be consumers and complementary factors of production in producing states, such as Texas, Louisiana, and Oklahoma, and foreign oil suppliers.

The argument that higher natural gas prices will not result in significantly greater supplies is contradicted by a number of serious studies by academicians and by oil companies. On the contrary, supplies can be expected to be far greater without cost-of-service price regulation, thus substantially reducing U.S. dependence on foreign oil supplies.

An artificial scarcity policy affecting both oil and gas resources is the system used to lease federal lands. It is estimated that most future petroleum resources will be found on these federal properties. The government has been extremely reluctant to permit Americans to make use of their own resources. In the future this policy will have to be drastically changed if domestic supplies are to approach their potential.

The only economical way out of the present energy dilemma is to allow energy markets to clear. If a free-market policy is not adopted, the shortages will tend to grow larger and supplies will dwindle. Or worse, the taxpayer will be called upon to contribute many tens of billions to subsidize federal energy corporations or the development of very high-cost unconventional sources.

APPENDIX A:
MEASURING ENERGY
CONSUMPTION AND PRICES

Aggregating an Energy Market: The Heat Approach

We have dealt with the primary fuel markets and with the degree of market overlap and inter-fuel competition. But many interesting and important questions make it necessary to aggregate these separate markets into an overall energy market. How fast is energy consumption growing? What is happening to energy prices? To answer these questions, we need a definition of energy and a unit of measurement. Those in the energy business measure oil in barrels, coal in tons, and natural gas in cubic feet. Since these are not comparable units, some common yardstick must be found.

The measure invariably used by energy researchers is the quantity of heat potentially derivable from a given quantity of a given fuel. The most common unit is the British thermal unit (btu), the quantity of heat necessary to raise the temperature of one pound of water one degree Fahrenheit. In these units a barrel of crude oil typically measures 5.8 million btus; a ton of coal, 24-28 million btus; and a cubic foot of gas, 1.03 thousand btus. Oil, coal, and gas can thus be added, subtracted, and otherwise statistically compared to ascertain energy consumption, production, and price patterns. The Bureau of Mines, Resources for the Future, the National Petroleum Council, and other energy research bodies have adopted this measure.[1]

In the past, in some parts of the energy market, this approach has served well. Consider what might be called the furnace or boiler-fuel market: industry, commercial establishments, electric utilities, and large residential units purchased fuels simply to burn them in furnaces

---

[1] See, for example, H. Landsberg and S. Schurr, *Energy in the United States: Sources, Uses, and Policy Issues* (New York: Random House, 1968).

to provide heat for offices and factories, to provide steam for industrial processes and electricity generation, or simply to heat water or space for apartment buildings. Although the handling, storage, and capital costs of oil, gas, and coal differed somewhat, as did the proportion of potential btus actually provided by the furnace, consumers of furnace fuels were in many cases interested primarily in purchasing btus, regardless of their form. They made their choice of which fuel to consume simply on the basis of the price per btu. In short, oil, coal, and gas were highly substitutable and highly competitive on a btu basis. Attesting to this fact is the close correlation between choice of fuel and average price per btu to electric power plants in different parts of the United States. Because of the locations of mines and wells and different transportation costs, delivered costs per btu of oil, coal, and gas will be different in various regions of the country. Invariably, electric plants chose to use the fuel that was cheapest per btu.[2]

The significance of this high degree of competitiveness and substitutability is that when we record someone using a btu of coal or a btu of oil, we are recording units of energy of a similar value to the user. The same can be said on the production or supply side, to the extent that markets are competitive. If marginal costs of delivering a btu of oil or coal or gas to the same point are equal, as they would be under competition, the economy gives up capital and labor resources of the same value whether a btu of oil or coal is delivered. Thus, under these conditions, btus of energy, whether in the form of oil or coal or gas, always mean the same thing in terms of marginal value to the consumer and marginal cost to the supplier.

While this situation may have prevailed to some extent in the furnace-fuel market for several decades, it never existed in some energy markets, does not exist in the boiler-fuel market today, and will not in the future. Take the gasoline market as an example. Historically a btu of gasoline has cost about twice as much as a btu of home heating oil. This is due not only to greater refining costs but in large part to greater distribution costs and taxes (which mostly go to pay for the use of public roads). Thus the value of a marginal btu of gasoline will be twice the value of a marginal btu of home heating oil. Adding together gasoline and heating oil btus is adding as equals things that are quite different from the point of the consumer.

---

[2] See Tables 1-14, p. 44, and 1-15, p. 45, in John Schanz and Helmut Frank, "Natural Gas in the Future Energy Pattern," in Brown, ed., *Regulation of the Natural Gas Producing Industry.*

The same is true from the point of view of the producer or supplier. It costs the economy more in labor and capital resources to supply a btu of gasoline than to supply a btu of heating oil. What sense does it make then to add them as if they were equal?

In short, gasoline is one kind of bundle of potential heat that is not the same to the consumer or the producer as other bundles of potential heat, much as an orange is not the same kind of bundle of citric acid as a grapefruit. We do not add oranges and grapefruits by their citric content to understand what is happening in the citric fruit market. That is because people buy citric fruits on the basis of properties other than their citric acid content. If we are to understand the energy market, we cannot add fuels as if their only physical property was the potential units of heat they can be converted to.

Where the heat approach gets into serious trouble is when it has to deal with electricity. An oil-fired electric generating plant uses roughly 11,400 btus of oil to deliver one kilowatt hour (kwh) of electricity to the consumer. But the kwh supplies only 3,400 btus to the consumer due to the waste of heat in generation and transmission. How many btus of energy do we record when one kwh is generated, 11,400 or 3,400? Viewed from the supply side, clearly 11,400 btus have been used up. But from the demand or consumer side only 3,400 are received. The answer has generally been to count the btus used up by primary suppliers rather than those delivered to consumers. The argument here would have to be that we are concerned only with heat used up and not with what the final consumer actually receives.

What happens then when we come to hydroelectric power, which is generated by the kinetic energy of falling water with no btus used? The approach has been to set down the number of btus that *would* have been used up had the electricity been generated by a coal-fired plant. Clearly this is inconsistent with the decision to measure btus used up rather than btus received by the final consumer.

This method of aggregating primary energy supplies—oil, gas, and coal—with secondary energy supplies—electricity and manufactured gas—using "heat" weights, either total btus used up, or btus consumed by the final consumer, is logically unsound and can lead to absurd statistical conclusions. R. Turvey and A. Nobay of the British Electricity Council found that the use of weights based on final consumption leads to the conclusion that nonindustrial energy consumption in the United Kingdom "*fell* by 3.6 percent from 1954 to 1964. Yet no one would seriously assert that fewer resources were used to provide domestic fuel and light in the latter year or that domestic consumers then had a lower standard of heating and lighting."[3] Apparently this quirk was due to the rapid growth of electricity, which provides more usable heat relative to btu potential than coal, which was declining as a heat source.

Suppose we concede that the electric power, motor vehicle transportation, and petrochemical sectors are ill suited to the use of heat weights. Can we not fall back to the position that within the boiler-fuel market the heat measure is appropriate and should at least be used there? Unfortunately, we can no longer answer affirmatively to this question. While one btu may have been as good as another in the past, this is not true today. The impact on air quality of burning fossil fuels has been introduced as a factor influencing the decision as to what fuel should be used. Sulfur oxides are a serious source of air pollution, and coal usually contains many times as much sulfur as low-sulfur heavy oil. Thus, in many places where coal could be supplied at a much lower cost than oil per btu, oil is used. Coal is not highly substitutable with oil today even in much of the boiler-fuel market.

The upshot of this discussion is that we cannot use heat units, or any other physical units, to measure a phenomenon that is essentially economic. Heat is supplied in every use of energy. But calories are supplied in every use of grain, and vitamin C in every use of citrus fruits. Yet we do not measure grain production in calories, or citrus fruit production in milligrams of vitamin C. We measure them by price-weighted indexes. In a free, competitive market relative prices will be proportional to relative consumer valuations at the margin and relative producer costs at the margin. Not all energy is traded in competitive markets. Electricity in all states must be sold by a regulated monopoly. Not all energy is traded in free markets. Natural gas prices are set well below the free-market level by the Federal Power Commission. Yet these deviations from the ideal are not fatal.

The deviation from free markets is serious, but it may be possible to statistically adjust for it. Despite problems in constructing price-weighted indexes, there is a strong presumption that they will give more sensible results. When Turvey and Nobay used price-weighted indexes in the U.K. several improvements over physical or heat indexes were observed. For example, we would expect an energy consumption index and the index of industrial production to be highly correlated. Taking first differences of all series, they found that the correlation between a heat index, such as that used in the U.S., and

[3] R. Turvey and A. Nobay, "On Measuring Energy Consumption," *The Economic Journal*, December 1965, p. 789.

industrial production was .67. The correlation between their price-weighted index and industrial production was .82.[4]

This suggests the possibility that some of the peculiar and unexplained phenomena in U.S. energy consumption may be less peculiar or more explainable if price weights are used. For example, would the sharp upturn in the ratio of U.S. energy consumption to gross national product occur in a price-weighted index? If so, would changes in relative prices of energy explain this shift?

Value-Weighted Indexes of U.S. Energy Consumption and Prices

The objective here is to measure the consumption and price of energy to the final consumer. For example, oil consumption in the form of gasoline must be distinguished from other forms and weighted according to consumer prices of gasoline. Heavy fuel oil consumption receives a much lower weight, since its price per gallon to the final user is lower. Heavy fuel oil prices are deflated by the wholesale price index (WPI), while gasoline prices are deflated by the consumer price index (CPI), because these commodities are sold in different markets. Heavy fuel oil consumed by electric utilities is not counted as final consumption. We measure electric power consumed weighted by its value and exclude all the oil, gas, and coal consumed in electric plants.

The classes of energy consumption and their weights based on 1960 values are:

Oil		63.0%
Gasoline	46.3%	
Distillates	13.7	
Heavy fuel oil (less utility use)	3.0	
Natural Gas		11.8
Residential	6.5	
Commercial	1.6	
Industrial (less utility use)	3.7	
Coal (less utility use)		2.9
Electricity		22.3
Residential	9.8	
Commercial	5.7	
Industrial	6.8	

[4] Ibid., p. 789.

Table A-1

INDEXES OF U.S. ENERGY CONSUMPTION, 1950–1970

(1960 = 100)

Year	Heat Index	Value-Weighted Index
1950	79	59
1955	89	81
1960	100	100
1965	120	125
1970	151	163

Source: U.S. Bureau of Mines and author.

Table A-2

AVERAGE ANNUAL ENERGY CONSUMPTION AND GROSS NATIONAL PRODUCT, RATES OF GROWTH, 1950–1970

	1950–55	1955–60	1960–65	1965–70
Heat index	3.4%	2.5%	3.9%	5.3%
Value-weighted index	7.7	4.6	4.9	6.2
Gross national product	4.7	2.3	5.3	3.4

Source: *Annual Report of the Council of Economic Advisers, 1973*, p. 194, and Table A-1.

The weights implicit in the heat index of consumption for 1960 are:

Oil	45.0%
Natural gas	28.5
Coal	22.8
Hydroelectric power	3.7

Nuclear power accounted for less than one-tenth of a percent.

It must be stressed that the value-weighted indexes are merely a first step toward better measurement of energy consumption and prices. A more detailed explanation of these statistics and their sources is given in the "Sources of Data" section of this appendix.

Table A-1 shows the heat index and the value-weighted index every five years from 1950 to 1970. The principal difference between the two series is that the value-weighted index grows faster in every period. This is shown even more clearly in Table A-2, where average annual rates of growth are given for each five-year period. Notice that this difference in rate of growth is much less pronounced after 1960.

The much heavier weight given to electricity and gasoline consumption in the value-weighted index accounts for most of the difference. Electricity consumption, in particular, grew much faster than nonelectric energy consumption over the whole period.

In general, the rates of growth in the two energy consumption indexes parallel the rates of growth of the real gross national product. The growth of both energy indexes slowed down in the 1955-1960 period when the growth rate of GNP slowed down, and then accelerated again when GNP grew faster from 1960 to 1965.

Only two cases diverged significantly from the parallel patterns of the economy and energy consumption. First, the value-weighted index grew exceptionally fast in the 1950-1955 period. Since the heat index did not, the answer must lie in the difference in weighting. The value-weighted index is much more sensitive to increased consumption of gasoline by automobiles and electricity by home appliances. Because of war-time shortage policies, there was enormous unmet demand for durable consumer goods, particularly automobiles and electrical appliances, in the immediate post-World War II years. From 1945 to 1950 consumer expenditures on durable goods rose at an average annual rate of 45 percent, while the real GNP was constant. It seems likely then that it is because electricity and gasoline consumption are more closely related to the stock of consumer durable goods than other forms of energy consumption that the value-weighted index showed a much higher growth rate than the heat index during the following five-year period.

Second, both energy consumption indexes accelerated during the 1965-1970 period, while the rate of growth of GNP slowed down, as compared to the previous five-year and ten-year periods. This is significant since it occurs in both energy indexes, indicating a general explanation and not a peculiarity of one index, and because it is in sharp contrast to the patterns of the previous fifteen years.

Much of the answer is to be found by looking at the value-weighted price index. Table A-3 shows the values of the index from 1950 to June 1973. Table A-4 shows the rates of change in the index. Energy prices have fallen dramatically since 1950 at a continuously accelerating rate of decline. The acceleration is particularly marked after 1960. Between 1960 and 1970 energy prices fell at more than twice the rate of decline from 1950 to 1960. If we consider that the consumer response to price takes time, probably several years because of the durability of energy-using equipment, the timing of the

Table A-3

VALUE-WEIGHTED INDEX OF ENERGY PRICES,
1950–JUNE 1973

(1960 = 100)

Year	Index
1950	107.2
1955	103.9
1960	100.0
1965	93.5
1970	85.4
June 1973	80.7

Source: Author.

Table A-4

AVERAGE ANNUAL RATE OF CHANGE OF ENERGY
PRICES, 1950–JUNE 1973

Period	Rate of Change
1950–55	−.62
1955–60	−.75
1960–65	−1.31
1965–70	−1.73
1970–June 1973	−1.87

Source: Author.

acceleration in consumption is readily interpreted. An accelerating rate of decline in energy prices induced an accelerating rate of growth in energy consumption.

This interpretation is reinforced by attempts to find factors that might have brought about exogenous shifts in the demand for energy after 1965. Even under very generous assumptions about what is an exogenous factor, it does not seem possible to ascribe the post-1965 acceleration to exogenous shifts in demand. The most ambitious attempt was made by Bruce Netschert who was able to account for only one-third of the acceleration in the heat index by factors such as the growth of air conditioning and the recent decline in electric plant efficiency, neither of which can be regarded as a truly exogenous development.[5]

From what we know of price elasticities of energy consumption, it is clear that the accelerating decline in energy prices can only be a partial explanation for the acceleration in consumption. The rate of price decline in the 1960-1965 period was only six-tenths of a percent per year greater than that of the 1950s, and the rate of decline from 1965 to 1970 was only seven-tenths of a percent per year greater than in the preceding ten years. Accounting completely for the 1.4 percent increase in the consumption growth rate (the 1965-1970 rate of 6.2 percent less the 1955-65 average of 4.8 percent) requires a price elasticity of demand of about -2.0. This is well above recent estimates of long-run elasticities of gasoline and electricity [6] and, of course, the overall price elasticity of energy must be smaller than the average elasticity of individual energy components. A careful econometric exercise would be required to say much more about this.

Sources of Data [7]

Total oil was divided into three groups—gasoline, which included motor and aviation fuel, kerosene, and jet fuel. Consumption data were taken from the United States Bureau of Mines *Minerals Year-book* (various editions). Gasoline prices used were taken from *Platt's Oilgram Price Service* and were deflated by the CPI.

The subdivision distillates include distillate oil, still gas, liquified gases, and the "miscellaneous" category of the *Minerals Yearbook*. Price data are those for Number 2 fuel oil as given by the U.S. Bureau of Labor Statistics, *Retail Prices and Indexes of Fuel and Utilities*. Prices for 1950 and 1955 were obtained by extrapolating 1960 figures backward at a rate of 3 percent lower in 1955 and 3 percent lower again for 1950. All were deflated by the CPI.

The subdivision heavy fuel oil includes residual fuel oil, lubricating oil, wax, coke, asphalt, and road oil. Quantities were obtained from the *Minerals Yearbook*. Prices from 1960 on were obtained from the National Coal Association's *Steam Electric Plant Factors*. Price

---

[5] National Economic Research Associates, "Energy Consumption and Gross National Product in the United States: An Examination of Recent Changes in the Relationship," privately circulated, March 1971.

[6] Houthakker and Verleger, "Dynamic Demand Analyses of Selected Energy Resources."

[7] Constance Boris assembled and computed all the data discussed in Appendix A. She has my gratitude for a job well done.

data for 1950 and 1955 were obtained from the New York Bunker "C" oil price series in early editions of the American Petroleum Institute's *Petroleum Facts and Figures* by a linking adjustment of .89 times the Bunker "C" prices. This adjustment factor was based on the normal relationship between the series where they overlapped historically. All heavy oil prices were deflated by the WPI.

Data on natural gas quantities and prices were obtained from various issues of the Bureau of Mines *Minerals Yearbook*. Residential and commercial prices were deflated by the CPI, while industrial prices were deflated by the WPI.

Coal consumption data were obtained from the *Minerals Yearbook*. Coal price data were obtained from *Steam Electric Plant Factors*. Prices for 1950 and 1955 were not available from this source. Prices for 1955 were therefore assumed to be the same as for 1956. Prices for 1950 were determined by taking the *Minerals Yearbook* f.o.b. mine values and calculating the average freight charge as the average difference between the f.o.b. mine value and the price at the electric power plant *(Steam Electric Plant Factors)* for 1956-60. All coal prices were deflated by the WPI.

Electric power consumption and price data were obtained from the Edison Electric Institute's *Statistical Yearbook* (various issues). Residential and commercial prices were deflated by the CPI, while industrial prices were deflated by the WPI.

Unpublished price data for 1971, 1972, and June 1973 were obtained from sources by telephone. Only natural gas and coal prices could not be obtained up to June 1973. Since these receive only a small weight in the overall price index they were extrapolated in the following way: Natural gas prices were extrapolated to June 1973 by assuming the same rate of increase as for 1971 and 1972. (The latter were obtained by telephone from the Bureau of Mines.) Coal prices for 1972 and June 1973 were obtained by extrapolating the rate of increase of 1970 to 1971.

APPENDIX B:
ON COMPETITION IN
THE PETROLEUM INDUSTRY

The main objective of petroleum policy is to provide the consumer with petroleum products at the lowest cost consistent with meeting demand. Obviously this objective is not being met. Supply is falling short of demand, and there is widespread suspicion that if past policies had been different, petroleum would be much more abundant today.

This suspicion is warranted. Public policy in the energy field has been deficient and has caused substantial injury to producers and consumers. Price controls on natural gas and oil, together with restrictive federal leasing policies, have created an energy crisis.

The subject of these hearings is the competitive market structure of the oil industry and possible reforms in that structure. The importance of this subject cannot be underestimated. The working of an efficient competitive market is fundamental to meeting our objectives of abundant supplies at lower costs. But we should be under no illusions regarding the role of competition in the present crisis. Imperfections in competitive structure have little to do with our current ills. Reforms in that structure will contribute little to resolving the problems consumers face today. Indeed, as is often the case with economic reforms, they may be disruptive in the short run even if beneficial in the long run. For these reasons we can indulge in a measure of deliberateness in these hearings that we could not afford in some other aspects of energy policy.

The focus of petroleum policy is the consumer. The optimal structure of the industry is the one that provides what he wants at the lowest possible price. The consumer could not care less whether

This statement is reprinted here substantially as presented by the author to the Special Subcommittee on Integrated Oil Operations, Committee on Interior and Insular Affairs, United States Senate, 21 February 1974.

the firms that supply him are large or small, integrated or noninte-grated, publicly run or privately owned. Whatever combination of industry characteristics results in the lowest costs in producing what he wants, and competes these low costs through to him, is the best system.

In assessing the present structure, these two questions are central: (1) are there features of the present structure that result in unnecessarily high costs, and (2) are all existing efficiencies passed on to the consumer, or are they retained as excess profits by suppliers? In my current study of the competitive structure, I have reached two preliminary conclusions: (1) some inefficiencies, traceable to government policies, have raised the cost of supplying petroleum, and (2) existing efficiencies are passed on to the consumer in the form of low prices. There are no excess profits.

Inefficiencies in the Petroleum Market

So long as the most efficient firm is allowed to do the job, the lowest costs will be realized. This will tend to occur in a free and open market. The search for inefficiencies is, therefore, largely a search for restrictions on the activities of firms.

The following inefficiencies exist in the petroleum market:

1. Because of price controls and the federal allocation system, supplies of crude oil and gasoline do not necessarily go to the firms and consumers that can offer the most for them and can make the best use of them. Refineries that would yield the most valuable products from a barrel of crude oil are not allocated the crude oil. Marketers that could more efficiently market gasoline are not allocated the gasoline. And finally consumers who might value a gallon of gasoline more than others do not receive it.

I have not attempted to quantify the distortions generated by price controls and governmental allocation, but it could be done fairly quickly, and the distortions might prove sizable. Americans returning from Europe remark at how much easier it is to buy gasoline in Europe than at home in spite of the fact that Europe is far more dependent on oil imported from boycotting producers. The few European countries that tried price controls and rationing quickly abandoned them, and the remainder ignored them from the start.

2. Current price controls on crude oil favor the small inefficient producer. The Trans-Alaska Pipeline Authorization Act of 1973 exempts from price ceilings wells producing less than ten barrels per day. In recent months this has meant a price for costly or "less

efficient" crude oil about double that for more economical crude. This may have an air of "fairness" about it, and I have no doubt that many regard this as reasonable. After all, if you have higher costs, should you not get a higher price?

The trouble with this policy is that it means higher costs, higher prices, and smaller supplies to the consumer. It means that $6.00 per barrel crude—the ceiling price is $5.25—cannot be produced, while $10.00 crude can. Furthermore, a stripper-well producer contemplating production of ten or fifteen barrels per day will find it more profitable to produce ten barrels at $10.00 than fifteen barrels at $5.25. (As one might expect, the price control rules do not allow the $10.00 price if one is producing less than the maximum feasible rate. But as a practical matter, there is no way of applying these restrictions to the more than 300,000 stripper wells throughout the United States.[1])

The upshot is that we are discouraging production of more economical crude in favor of more costly crude and getting less oil in the end. It has been argued that we are favoring small business and *thereby* promoting competition. We are certainly favoring small business. But we are obviously *curtailing* competition and making oil more scarce.

3. The Federal Power Commission regulation of natural gas prices has for more than a decade created enormous distortions in the energy market. Natural gas is selling for an average of about eighteen cents per million btus, while crude oil from abroad sells for almost ten times that much. The economic waste from this policy is readily calculable, given assumptions about supply and demand elasticities of natural gas and other fuels. By the most conservative assumptions the nation is wasting billions of dollars per year in scarce capital and labor resources, and, by creating an unnecessary reliance on foreign oil, reducing the international exchange value of the dollar. Millions of consumers of home heating oil would be either heating with cheaper natural gas or cheaper home heating oil were it not for this policy.

Just as with crude oil, natural gas prices are not regulated in the case of smaller producers. The Federal Power Commission exempts firms producing less than 10 billion cubic feet per year from price regulation, resulting in the same kind of distortion as with crude oil production.

4. The Department of the Interior in disposing of royalty oil from OCS leases does not sell it to the highest bidder but allocates

---

[1] The rules are contained in the Code of Federal Regulations, Title 10, Part 210.31-32.

almost all of it to small refiners. Royalty oil from inland federal leases is also allocated disproportionately to small refiners. Again, this may help small business, but it reduces competition and creates inefficiency.

5. In the past enormous inefficiencies were created in some major producing states by the system of market-demand prorationing. Under this system small inefficient wells were allowed to produce without output limitations while efficient wells were required to cut back production substantially. In 1965, a costly stripper well capable of producing ten barrels per day in Texas was allowed to produce ten barrels per day while an efficient flush well might have been allowed as little as 28 percent of its potential production. To cover the high cost of production from the inefficient wells, prices had to be higher, and to sustain these higher prices, production had to be cut back on efficient wells, thereby artificially raising their production costs.

6. The mandatory oil import quotas established in 1959 discriminated against large refiners in favor of small refiners. Licenses to import oil from overseas were distributed to refiners on the basis of refinery throughput and a so-called "sliding scale." In 1969, for example, refiners with throughput of 10,000 barrels per day received licenses to import 1,950 barrels per day—or 19.5 percent—while refiners with throughput of 500,000 barrels per day received licenses for imports of 21,050 barrels per day—or 4.2 percent. Since these licenses were valued in the market at about $1.25 per barrel, the small refiner received a subsidy of 24.4 cents per barrel of throughput while the larger refiner received a subsidy of only 5.3 cents.

Elementary economics tells us that a uniform subsidy will tend to be passed through to consumers, while any special subsidies to particular firms will go either to offset inefficient operations or into the pockets of the small refiner as excess profit. Thus, the consumer would be better off if licenses had been distributed on a proportional basis.

Neither the oil import quotas nor market-demand limitations on crude oil production exist today. Production allowables in Texas reached 100 percent in April 1972, and a year later oil import quotas were scrapped.

7. Under the new oil import program launched by the President in April 1973 quotas have been dropped, but a small license fee—a euphemism for tariff—has been placed on crude oil and more substantial license fees have been placed on products. Some crude, however, may be imported without payment of a fee. These fee-exempt

licenses will be allocated to refiners on the same kind of sliding-scale basis used under the old oil import program. Thus the differential subsidy to small refiners continues, and with it inefficiencies and/or windfalls. Under the plan announced by the President these fee-exempt licenses will be phased out by 1980.

In citing these inefficiencies, I am not suggesting that all of the programs and policies that created them were unwise. In some cases, such as the oil import program, the inefficiency cited was a minor aspect of the program and a judgment about the overall value of the program would require analysis of many other aspects. In other cases, such as regulation of natural gas prices, the inefficiency mentioned was a major consequence of the policy. Also, there is no presumption that these inefficiencies are of the same order of magnitude. For example, the inefficiencies caused by the biased allocation of royalty oil are probably much smaller than the others.

In spite of all the qualifications that have to be made, there is still a definite public policy theme underlying all but two of these inefficiencies: the policy was motivated by concern for small business. To the extent that these policies are justified by the rationale that the assistance of small business is socially desirable for its own sake, one can only urge that the full costs of achieving this objective be weighed against its value. Consumers are suffering, and we had better be sure that their suffering is not too high a price to pay for this objective. Also, there are much simpler ways of subsidizing small business without creating significant market distortions. Finally, I would point out that many of these "small" businesses are firms worth tens of millions of dollars.

To the extent these policies are justified by the rationale that by promoting small business we are promoting competition and thus lowering consumer prices, the policies are seriously mistaken. In each of the cases cited, the small business subsidy curtails competition and results in higher costs and prices.

Competition, Entry and Profits

Three decades of congressional hearings on the petroleum markets have attempted to identify small business and competition. To a great extent they have established this connection in the public mind. We are told that there are twenty giant oil companies in the petroleum industry and a large number of small companies that provide them with some competition. These twenty giant companies "control" production, refining, transportation, and marketing sectors of the industry. This "handful" of twenty giant companies form an "oligopoly," a notion that makes my dictionary pitifully obsolete.

There is no systematic evidence that the petroleum industry is not highly competitive as it stands. There is no evidence that it would be substantially less competitive if the numerous small firms disappeared. (It would certainly be less efficient, since many small firms are very efficient. On the other hand, some small firms exist only by virtue of the aforementioned subsidies.)

The belief that small firms and less concentration are needed is based on the theory that the larger firms systematically exclude smaller firms from the industry, and therefore prices are not driven down to costs (including normal return on capital). This theory has one clear implication: if prices are not driven down to costs, then monopoly or excess profits will be made by the large companies.[2] Indeed many economists have regarded profitability as the premier test of monopoly.[3] Nevertheless, the connection between monopoly and profits is a highly qualified one. Perhaps the strongest statement that can be made is that the persistence of abnormally high profits over long periods of time in a particular industry make it more likely that the industry is monopolistic than competitive.[4]

Note the three qualifications in the statement: First, the statement is probabilistic. High profits are not a sure indicator of monopoly. Competitive industries earn high profits when favorable unanticipated shifts in demand and supply occur, and monopolies can earn normal or below-normal profits when unfavorable, unanticipated shifts occur. Second, the statement refers to the persistence of high profits over a long period of time. The larger the time span, the more likely that high profits are due to monopoly as opposed to favorable market conditions: the probability of perpetual good fortune is infinitesimal. Third, the statement refers to industry profits, not company profits.[5]

---

[2] Note that the special features of the petroleum industry—market-demand prorationing, import quotas, price regulation of natural gas, the depletion allowance—do not have long-run effects on the rate of profit in the industry because they do not affect entry into the industry. Those that make prices higher or costs lower merely attract more firms into the industry until prices fall or costs rise, or both, and profits fall to normal. Those that make prices lower, such as natural gas price regulation, drive firms out of the industry until profits rise to normal levels.

[3] Fritz Machlup, *The Political Economy of Monopoly* (Baltimore: The Johns Hopkins University Press, 1952).

[4] J. S. Bain, "The Profit Rate as a Measure of Monopoly Power," *The Quarterly Journal of Economics*, vol. 42, no. 2 (February 1941), p. 274.

[5] Yale Brozen, "Significance of Profit Data for Antitrust Policy," in J. Fred Weston and Sam Peltzman, eds., *Public Policy Toward Mergers* (Pacific Palisades, Calif.: Goodyear, 1969), p. 113.

Monopoly profits are due to higher prices which in turn are brought about by curtailed output. All firms in an industry benefit from higher prices, not just those that curtail output. (The requirement that excess profits be long-lived to indicate monopoly suggests the absurdity of recent claims that high oil company accounting profits recorded in the last quarter of 1973 demonstrate a conspiracy or monopoly power. Profits of one quarter or one year or even a few years provide no evidence regarding monopoly. Furthermore, there was a clearly unanticipated supply shift favorable to industry profits: the Arab oil boycott brought on by the October Arab-Israeli war.)

When we turn to measuring long-term profitability, we are faced with two alternatives: accounting measures derived from balance sheets and profit and loss statements, and realized profits to the stockholder as measured by stock price appreciation and dividends paid. Accounting measures of profits suffer a number of serious defects because accounting conventions are only vaguely related to economic theory. Expenditures that should be capitalized, such as advertising and research and development, frequently are not. Depreciation charges usually reflect simple arithmetic rules rather than actual changes in the value of assets. Future income not yet confirmed by sales contracts is ignored. Even without these problems, the procedure of estimating the rate of return on capital by the ratio of income to stockholders' equity or invested capital can give widely disparate answers for a given true rate of return depending upon the particular time pattern of cash flows.[6] Finally, we must hope that the accountants have not imputed capital values to any future monopoly profits acquired by the firm at times of organization, merger, or acquisition.

The alternative approach is more closely related to the economist's conception of profit. If a firm that is worth $100 million at the beginning of the year is worth $120 million at the end of the year, there has been a profit of $20 million, and the firm has earned 20 percent on its capital investment. Instead of attempting to estimate the true value of the firm from accounting records, we observe the value the market places on the firm. After all, buyers and sellers of shares of the firm have access not only to accounting statements, but to all kinds of other facts that affect valuation. The importance of this other information is indicated by the fact that the market value of a share of stock of a company is usually very different from the ac-

[6] E. Solomon, "Alternative Rate of Return Concepts and Their Implication for Utility Regulation," *Bell Journal of Economics and Management Science*, vol. 1, no. 1 (Spring 1970).

countant's book value of a share of stock. This is particularly important in the producing sector of the petroleum industry where there are enormous discrepancies between the value of oil discovered and the dollar value of capital assets used in the search for that oil.

If we engage in the following procedure, we will not miss any profits the firm has realized, and we will measure the actual rate of return to a stockholder. Take the price of a company's stock at a beginning point in time; invest all dividends back into the firm by buying shares at the market price after the dividends have been paid; then calculate the wealth of the stockholder at the ending time point, a wealth increased by virtue of price appreciation and the greater number of shares due to reinvestment of dividends. We will not have missed any profits to the company because profits must be either paid out in dividends or used by the firm to purchase new assets, and these assets will enhance the market value of the firm and be reflected in stock prices. (We ignore any additional executive compensation paid out of profits as being too small to be concerned about for the large firms we will be dealing with.) Therefore, there can be no fear that some kind of financial sleight-of-hand has removed from the figures profits that are really there.

The rate of return calculated is simply the annual rate of return, which, if realized every year, would result in the same increase in wealth as experienced by the stockholder. The stockholder does not, of course, experience the same increase in wealth each year. The calculated rate of return must therefore be interpreted as an average.

One criticism of this approach is that initial period stock prices may already capitalize expected future monopoly profits. Therefore, rates of return calculated on initial stock prices would only reflect normal rates of return, even though monopoly profits were being earned. (Note that a similar criticism applies to accounting profits since book values may include some capitalized monopoly profits.)

As a practical matter this probably has little effect on our calculated rates of return. Any monopoly profits earned in the petroleum industry would—even industry critics would agree—require lax antitrust and regulatory policy and a passive Congress and executive. The uncertainty of future public policy would mean that these monopoly profits would be discounted at a very high rate and that monopoly profits that might accrue four or five years in the future would be accorded a very small value in present stock prices. If we are dealing with a period of twenty years, the influence of capitalized profits of a few years should be very small. Monopoly profits earned continuously for a couple of decades should definitely show up in our figures.

When my study is completed, it will deal with both accounting and market-related measures of profitability. At the present time only the market data have been adequately analyzed. The Standard and Poor's COMPUSTAT tapes available at the University of Michigan contain accounting and market data on oil corporations listed on the New York Stock Exchange and American Stock Exchange from 1953 to 1972. Only twenty-three petroleum companies were listed on these exchanges for the entire period. By also considering the period 1960 to 1972, it was possible to expand the number of petroleum companies to forty-nine.

As a standard of reference or norm, the rate of return of the Standard and Poor's (S&P) 500 stock composite index was calculated. The results for forty-nine petroleum companies and for the S&P composite are shown in Table B-1. (The classification of petroleum companies and the exclusion of some companies from the list would require considerable discussion. The basic principle of exclusion was that a company must have a majority of its assets in petroleum or a majority of its earnings from petroleum to be considered a petroleum company. Companies such as Tenneco, Penzoil, and Signal, which are primarily in nonpetroleum businesses, were excluded. Natural gas pipeline transportation and contract drilling were not considered part of the "petroleum industry" as defined here.)

Some of the significant conclusions to emerge from these figures are:

1. American petroleum companies were significantly less profitable than the S&P 500 over the 1953 to 1972 period. Indeed, not one of the twenty-one American petroleum companies equalled the S&P 500's rate of return!

2. The eight companies charged by the Federal Trade Commission with monopolizing the industry earned an average rate of return of 12.1 percent, more than 20 percent below the S&P norm for the 1953 to 1972 period.

3. Canadian and overseas producers were far more profitable than domestic producers, domestic refiners, or internationals, and significantly more profitable than the S&P 500. Canadian refiners were much closer to the norm.

4. Domestic refining was far more profitable than domestic production over the 1960-1972 period, and based on just two domestic producers, was more profitable over the whole 1953-72 period.

Table B-1

OIL INDUSTRY STOCKHOLDERS' AVERAGE ANNUAL RATE OF RETURN[a] AND STANDARD & POOR'S 500 STOCK COMPOSITE INDEX, 1953–72 AND 1960–72

Refiners	1953–72	1960–72	Producers	1953–72	1960–72
Domestic			**Domestic**		
American Petrofina	—	18.5%	Aztec	—	8.9%
Ashland	13.8%	13.6	Baruch-Foster	—	0.9
Atlantic Richfield	12.8	14.6	Consolidated	—	4.9
Cities Service	10.5	9.7	Crestmont	—	−4.8
Clark	—	19.0	Crystal	—	4.8
Commonwealth	—	11.8	Felmont	—	8.7
Continental	9.0	6.9	General American	8.9%	11.5
Crown	—	9.0	Louisiana Land	—	13.7
Getty	12.3	16.0	Superior	9.0	8.9
Husky	—	11.4	Westates	—	5.5
Kerr-McGee	14.6	18.3			
Marathon	9.7	10.2	Average	9.0%	6.3%
Murphy	—	10.5			
Phillips	9.4	7.8	**Canadian**		
Reserve	—	−5.2	Canadian Export	—	6.4%
Shell	9.9	6.8	Canadian Homestead	—	24.9
Skelly	10.2	12.5	Canadian Superior	—	14.3
Standard (Indiana)	11.7	15.3	Dome	21.4%	32.0
Standard (Ohio)	15.4	16.1	Home	—	15.8
Sun	7.1	9.4	United Canso	—	20.3
Union	11.1	12.8			
			Average	21.4%	19.0%
Average	11.3%	11.7%			
			Overseas		
International			Asamera	—	37.5%
Exxon	11.6%	10.7%	Belco	—	4.7
Gulf	12.3	8.9	Creole	—	5.2
Mobil	13.3	15.3	Occidental	—	23.8
Standard (Cal.)	11.4	10.2			
Texaco	13.7	9.7	Average	—	17.8%
Average	12.5%	11.0%			
Canadian					
Gulf Oil of Canada	—	11.1%			
Imperial Oil	12.4%	17.2			
Pacific Petroleum	—	12.3			
Average	12.4%	13.5%			

Standard & Poor's 500 Stock Composite Index

1953–72	15.6
1960–72	12.8

[a] Annual rate of return that would yield same increase in value over the period as realized price appreciation with dividends reinvested. Figures shown are averages of three rates of return based on three alternative price assumptions: (1) Stock purchased at initial year's high, sold at final year's high, with all dividends reinvested at succeeding year's high, (2) stock purchased at initial year's low, sold at final year's low, with dividends reinvested at succeeding year's low, and (3) stock purchased at initial year's closing price, sold at final year's closing price, with dividends reinvested at succeeding year's closing price.

From 1960 to 1972 domestic producers realized less than half the rate of return of the S&P 500.

These figures provide strong evidence that no excess profits were earned by domestic petroleum companies and thus contradict the theses that firms have been deterred from entering the petroleum industry and that prices are above costs.[7] The immediate task for economists is to explain why the industry has been so unprofitable and why capital continued to flow in. That explanation will not be attempted here.

If the exclusionary thesis is wrong, then there must be something wrong with the logic of that thesis or with certain key factual assumptions. To examine the thesis, I will set out an oversimplified version. Any version must be oversimplified because the charges against the larger petroleum companies are so numerous, so varied, and often so contradictory, that it would take a dissertation just to sort them out.

First, it is usually asserted that the industry is dominated by a small number of firms. In the economist's jargon, it is concentrated. This, it is alleged, permits monopoly power.

Second, it is alleged that the high degree of vertical integration further enhances this monopoly power. One of the most popular theses asserts that refining margins are artificially low and crude prices artificially high because of the favored tax treatment of production. This makes it impossible for firms to enter refining without integrating into production and thus raises further barriers to entry. (This argument seems to have been developed by Melvin de Chazeau and Alfred Kahn and has been used by the Federal Trade Commission and Professors Fred Allvine and G. Patterson—the latter, in these hearings—and in numerous popular pieces.) Small marketers are injured because there are fewer small refiners to purchase gasoline from and because the larger companies will not sell to them.

Third, refiners and small marketers are further excluded or handicapped by the fact that crude and product pipelines are overwhelmingly owned by large companies either singly or in joint ventures.

While I would like to deal with all of these theses, my research on the marketing and pipeline sectors is too preliminary to be used

---

[7] I have examined the question of whether it is possible that capitalized monopoly profits formed so large a part of the initial year's price that they masked a monopoly rate of return on the competitive value of assets. For the FTC Eight it turns out that for monopoly profits to have been earned, capitalized monopoly profits must have accounted for an overwhelming portion of 1953 market value, an implication that cannot be reconciled with the 1953 accounting data on assets.

here. However, there does appear to be an enormous amount of data to test theses regarding exclusion and cartelization. Considering the widespread charges, it is surprising that no systematic analyses have been carried out.

Consider the issue of concentration: In the first place, after an enormous amount of statistical research, there appears to be little, if any, correlation between concentration and monopoly profits across industries.[8] Thus concentration does not offer even a presumption of monopoly. Second, the petroleum industry is not highly concentrated: The average market share of the four largest firms for all U.S. manufacturing industries in 1966 was 39 percent.[9] In 1972 the four largest domestic refiners had less than 33 percent of the market, and the four largest domestic crude oil producers had 31 percent of the market.[10] In 1968 the four largest natural gas producers had 25 percent of the interstate market.[11] Most manufacturing industries are more concentrated than the petroleum industry.

Perhaps no other aspect of the petroleum industry has brought more confused discussion than vertical integration. The theory of vertical integration is simple: firms internalize operations when it is more economical than using the marketplace.[12] Indeed, the business firm itself is the first step in vertical integration. One would think therefore than an inquiry into vertical integration would focus on the economies that can be obtained by bringing certain market transactions within the firm. Surprisingly, the high degree of vertical integration in the petroleum industry has spurred a search for devious explanations.

The most popular thesis is that developed by de Chazeau and Kahn,[13] and can be summarized as follows: A firm that had crude production equal to its refinery output would be indifferent to the

---

[8] H. Demsetz, *The Market Concentration Doctrine* (Washington, D.C.: American Enterprise Institute, 1973).

[9] William G. Shepherd, *Market Power and Economic Welfare: An Introduction* (New York: Random House, 1970), p. 106.

[10] The *Oil and Gas Journal* staff, American Petroleum Institute, and U.S. Bureau of Mines.

[11] Federal Power Commission, *Sales by Producers of Natural Gas to Interstate Pipe Lines* (Washington, D. C.: Government Printing Office, 1969).

[12] R. Coase, "The Nature of the Firm," *Economica*, vol. 9 (1937), pp. 386-405.

[13] Melvin G. de Chazeau and Alfred Kahn, *Integration and Competition in the Petroleum Industry* (New Haven: Yale University Press, 1959), pp. 221-229. The opposite of this thesis was put forward by Eugene Rostow in *A National Policy for the Oil Industry* (New Haven: Yale University Press, 1948), and is now being examined by a committee of the California legislature. This is but one illustration of the contradictory nature of the charges against the industry.

price of crude oil for a given product price. Its total revenues would be the same regardless of the crude price and, given its costs, its profits would be the same. However, crude production is favored by the tax system. Higher crude prices mean a greater value to the depletion allowance and, thus, lower taxes. Thus, for any product price and profit before taxes, a greater profit after taxes can be realized by taking minimum earnings on refinery operations and maximum earnings in crude production.

Few refiners have complete self-sufficiency in crude production. But even if they have a fairly high degree of self-sufficiency, it can be shown arithmetically that they will benefit from a rise in crude prices even if product prices remain unchanged. When the depletion allowance was 27.5 percent, a refiner with 77 percent self-sufficiency or higher would benefit from higher crude prices even if product prices remained unchanged. If only a part of the crude price increase were passed on in the product price, a correspondingly lower degree of self-sufficiency would suffice to make the crude price increase profitable. (The FTC's report on the petroleum industry succeeds in proving the impossible: that the reduction in the depletion allowance increases the incentive to higher crude prices!) [14]

Thus, an artificially high crude price and artificially low refining margin will exist. This makes it difficult for refiners that are not integrated to survive and discourages entry into refining since the refiner must also be a crude producer.

This artificial price structure obviously implies that crude production will be more profitable than refining, and therefore both crude producers and highly self-sufficient refiners will be more profitable than less integrated refiners. In fact, de Chazeau and Kahn show that from 1947 to 1957 security prices of producers and highly self-sufficient refiners substantially outperformed less integrated refiners. Also, from 1946 to 1955 accounting profits on total invested capital were higher for producers than for refiners. [15]

This argument is not sustainable in logic or in fact. It is true that artificially small refining margins would drive nonintegrated refiners out of the business. However, they would also drive integrated refiners out of the refining business. If the refining business is unprofitable, it is unprofitable to everyone. The argument requires integrated

---

14 This is due to an arithmetic error. See *Preliminary Federal Trade Commission Staff Report on its Investigation of the Petroleum Industry* (Washington, 1973), Appendix B. I am grateful to my colleague, Richard Mancke, for pointing this out and the fact that when the arithmetic is corrected, the argument collapses.

15 Ibid., pp. 321-332.

refiners to continue investing in activities that yield subnormal earnings and thus not to maximize the total profits of the firm. The rational integrated firm would cease investing in refineries and invest in super-profitable crude production. Indeed, anyone, whether refiner, producer, or outside the oil business, would want to invest in production and avoid refining. Thus, capital would continue to flow into production and avoid refining until each sector's rate of return became normal and equal.

But, it will be counter-argued, this is a conspiracy, and even though it is not rational for the individual firm to build refineries, the group must build them and so they will be built. Adding the assumption of conspiracy does make the argument more logical, but it makes it even less realistic. If a cartel is requiring its members to invest in unprofitable activities, then it must divide this burden among the firms in some equitable manner. But, in fact, refining and production activities—that is, unprofitable and profitable activities—are shared very unequally among large firms. Getty's ratio of crude oil production to refinery runs in 1972 was 149 percent. Standard of Ohio's ratio was 7 percent. How does Getty induce Standard of Ohio to keep sinking money into refineries? For this cartel to work, literally billions of dollars of bribes would have to be paid among the top twenty or so companies. No evidence has been presented that this happens. To my knowledge, no one has suggested that it happens.

What about refining and producing profits? Everyone knows that producing is more profitable than refining. As with so many things everyone knows, this is untrue. During the period examined by de Chazeau and Kahn (1947-1957) crude prices rose 64 percent. During the same period spare capacity in refining rose from 4.9 percent to 10.1 percent. It would certainly be surprising if stock prices of producers had not performed better than those of refiners.

Economic theory suggests that production and refining should be equally profitable in the long run, although they may certainly differ in the short run. Therefore, over the long run producers should earn rates of return similar to refiners, and refiners with relatively large crude production should earn rates of return similar to less integrated refiners.

Looking back at Table B-1 we find only two producers for the period 1953 to 1972, and they earned 9 percent. Fourteen refiners averaged 11.3. It would be hard to say profitability was significantly different given only two observations on producers. In any case it certainly contradicts the de Chazeau-Kahn thesis which requires that the producers do better than the refiners. When we turn to the 1960-

1972 data, we find ten producers averaging 6.3 percent, much lower than the twenty-one-refiner average of 11.7 percent.

To compare profitability of more integrated and less integrated refiners, I have plotted the rates of return against the so-called "self-sufficiency ratio," the volume of crude production divided by refinery runs. Figure B-1 shows the 1953 to 1972 period, and Figure B-2 shows the 1960 to 1972 period. In both cases there is an absence of correlation. The most profitable firms include crude-poor and crude-rich refiners.

The notion that vertical integration is a device by which large firms monopolize the industry is also inconsistent with some other facts. For one thing large companies are not especially integrated as compared to small companies. The most recent analysis of the degree of integration of large and small firms was done for 1960. In that year the twenty largest domestic refiners had an average ratio of crude production to refinery runs of 49.7 percent. Of the next twenty-five largest refiners, only eighteen offered data adequate to calculate this ratio, and the average ratio for these eighteen refiners was 44 percent.[16] And a comprehensive survey of refiners in 1950 showed that refiners that were totally nonintegrated accounted for less than 2 percent of U.S. refinery capacity.[17] The notion that there is a group of "independent" refiners significantly less integrated than "major" refiners is apparently a myth.

Have small firms been deterred from entering the refining business? The FTC has explicitly stated that barriers to entry into refining are "overwhelming" and that "there has been virtually no new entry into the industry."[18]

It is difficult to find a good yardstick for ease of entry, but perhaps the simplest approach is just to count how many firms have entered and relate the number to the size of the industry. The Bureau of Mines survey of refineries for 1972 indicates that thirty-one refiners had capacities of 50,000 barrels per day or greater. In 1951 the number was twenty. Nine of these thirty-one companies were not in the refining business in 1950 and ten of the fourteen newcomers (three 1950 companies merged with others in the top twenty) entered by

[16] Statement of Morris Livingston before the U.S. District Court for the Northern District of California, Southern Division, in the case of United States of America v. Standard Oil Co. (Indiana), Civil No. 40212.

[17] John McLean and Robert Haigh, *The Growth of Integrated Oil Companies* (Washington, D. C.: Howard University Press, 1954).

[18] Testimony of James T. Halverson of the Federal Trade Commission before the Subcommittee on Antitrust and Monopoly of the Senate Judiciary Committee, 27 June 1973, pp. 21-25.

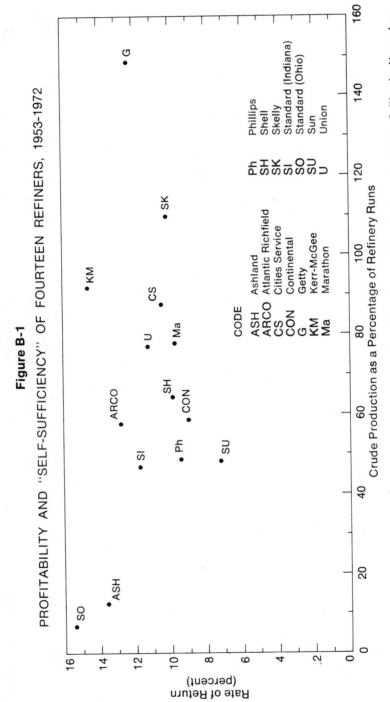

Figure B-1

PROFITABILITY AND "SELF-SUFFICIENCY" OF FOURTEEN REFINERS, 1953-1972

Rate of Return (percent)

Crude Production as a Percentage of Refinery Runs

CODE
ASH   Ashland
ARCO   Atlantic Richfield
CS   Cities Service
CON   Continental
G   Getty
KM   Kerr-McGee
Ma   Marathon

Ph   Phillips
SH   Shell
SK   Skelly
SI   Standard (Indiana)
SO   Standard (Ohio)
SU   Sun
U   Union

Source: Profit data is from Table B-1; self-sufficiency data is from *Rice/Kerr Chemical Service* (Laguna Beach, California, November 1972).

Figure B-2

PROFITABILITY AND "SELF-SUFFICIENCY" OF NINETEEN REFINERS, 1960–1972

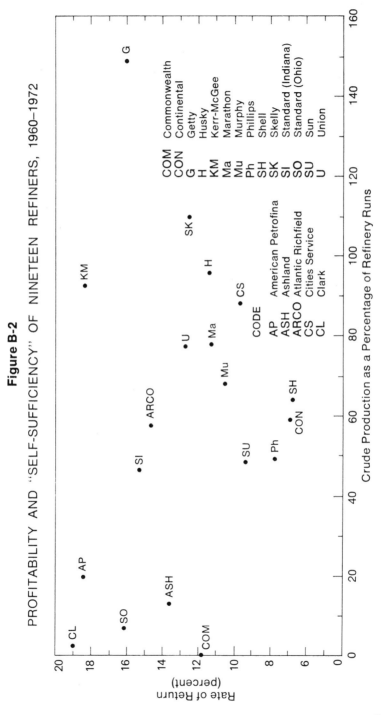

Source: Profit data is from Table B-1; self-sufficiency data is from *Rice/Kerr Chemical Service* (Laguna Beach, California, November 1972).

building totally new capacity—not by purchasing existing refineries.[19] While it is hard to construct an absolute standard for ease of entry, the fact that 30 percent of the larger refiners in 1972 were not in the refining business in 1950 does not suggest "overwhelming" barriers to entry.

Why then are petroleum companies so integrated? There seem to be three major reasons. First, there are economies of management. Each stage of the industry—production, refining, transportation, and marketing—is highly dependent upon the others. The success of a refinery is more a function of success in the raw materials and product markets than of success in refinery operations. It is apparently more efficient in many circumstances to plan jointly corollary and supporting investments than to rely on other firms at other stages to make the right investments at the right time in the right place. This is not to say that other firms could not make these investments, but rather that they will make them less efficiently.

A second motive for integration is the reduction in variability of profits. When a petroleum company finds itself with additional funds for investment, beyond what can profitably be used in its own sector, it seeks out investments whose returns are not highly correlated with the company's main business so as to stabilize earnings. Remarkably, it happens that the profitability of the production, refining, and marketing sectors of the petroleum industry are not highly correlated with one another. Over the period 1920 to 1952 John McLean and Robert Haigh found that a nonintegrated mid-continent refiner would have average monthly fluctuations in gross margins four times the size of a fully integrated refiner. Substantial stabilization of earnings were also shown for producers and marketers who integrated.

A third reason for integration is to assure "availability" of supplies. In a few cases a refinery may be geared to process a very special type of crude for which the market is thin. Integration will assure supplies at relatively constant costs. But most refineries are equipped to process a range of crudes that are sold in active markets. This permits them to outbid rivals for limited supplies. What probably motivates a concern for availability here is the fear of price controls. Petroleum prices were controlled in World War II, in the Korean War, and since 1971 under the President's New Economic Program. At other times informal government pressure has been placed on petroleum companies to hold prices down. Judging by the spurts in crude prices when these controls have been relaxed, we must conclude that

---

[19] National Petroleum Refiners Association, *Washington Bulletin*, 29 June 1973, p. 2.

the shortages created were large and that the value of crude oil substantially exceeded the ceiling price. Since the probability of price control, formal or informal, has remained high in recent decades, it is not surprising to find businessmen providing for the eventuality. Since the FPC regulation of natural gas prices in the 1960s, pipeline companies have been integrating backward into production. The recent controls on crude oil prices have motivated firms as diverse as Bethelehem Steel, Ryder Systems, and Dow Chemical to move into crude oil and natural gas production. The list also includes General Motors, Ford, International Paper, St. Regis Paper and W. R. Grace. By internalizing the sale of crude oil within the firm, these companies can avoid the problem of price controls. Given price controls, this is a socially useful response, but it is of course far less efficient than simply removing the price controls.

Conclusions

The consumer is best served when (1) the petroleum industry is efficiently organized and the lowest costs of supply are realized, and (2) the benefits of these low costs are passed through to the consumer by competition. The consumer wants an efficient and a competitive industry.

Some inefficiencies in the petroleum market exist and are traceable to government policies. An important theme running through many of these policies is an attempt to favor or assist small business.

Prices paid by consumers for petroleum products reflect the actual costs of suppliers and are not "padded" by excess profits. The competitive process has held industry profits down. The petroleum industry over the past two decades has, in fact, earned subnormal profits.

Cover and book design: Pat Taylor